DARK NIGHT

Reclaiming the Discarded Other
on the Journey to Wholeness

Susan Wright, Ed.D.

TCP Publications

Vancouver Canada

TPC Publications
314 – 525 Wheelhouse Square
Vancouver, BC V5Z 4L8
www.thecoachingproject.com

Library and Archives Canada Cataloguing in Publication

Wright, Susan Janet, author

Dark Night: reclaiming the discarded other on the journey to wholeness / Susan Wright

Includes bibliographical references.

ISBN: 978-0-9733260-3-1

Wright, Susan Janet, Life Transition. 2. Psychology.
3. Personal Growth. I. Title

Artwork: S. Wright
Editing: Lucidedit.com
Graphics: Limina.ca

DARK NIGHT

Reclaiming the Discarded Other
on the Journey to Wholeness

Contents

PART THREE: ACCOMPLISHING THE PASSAGE

Acknowledgements

I want to express my deepest gratitude to all those who suffered through my dark night with me. Family, friends and colleagues, I thank you from the bottom of my heart.

These same dear ones and many others have encouraged me to tell my story and share it with the world. I am forever in your debt – early readers, generous editors, and spirit boosters.

A special appreciation to my courageous friends who have allowed me to tell their dark night stories. The book is much richer for your involvement, and so am I.

Finally, to Carol for being my amanuensis to the finish line, and Femi for his loving support and patience with the many hours at my desk.

Preface

We have to drink the stupefying cup of darkness
and wake up to ourselves, nourished and surprised.
*... **Edward Hirsch***

It's strange really, because I'm such a happy person.
I've led a life of privilege—no trauma, abuse or deprivation.
I've always felt enspirited and energetic, curious and
passionate, loving and loved. I'm ceaselessly optimistic and
see my life as a relatively easy ride so far with pretty much
everything turning out well. I have alternately climbed the
corporate and educational ladders and have been a leader in
both. In my early sixties I had the resources to withdraw
from professional work and create the life I wanted for the
rest of my days. The question is: why did I fall into a deep
well of darkness, grief and despair that took roughly five
years to crawl out of?

I've thought endlessly about this question but for the
first time ever, my thinking hasn't done me much good. I
can't think my way through what happened; it's not that
kind of experience.

There is a natural turning inward as life progresses, a
reflective review of what's behind and what's ahead,
acknowledging limitations and facing the reality of death,
sensing the presence of the infinite. As we transition from

stage to stage in our growth as adults, we may experience feelings of disruption and confusion. But that doesn't begin to describe the process of losing my identity, my bearings, everything I believed in and counted on, with nothing to replace it, simply to drift with no control in the blackness, like being stranded in space with no hope of returning to all that once was true.

That undoubtedly sounds like an overly dramatic description. What I experienced wasn't like deep depression, a melancholy where one not only feels persistently sad but also experiences changes in sleep, appetite and concentration, or has thoughts of suicide. No, it's more like a mist gradually rolls in, a foreboding, bringing with it a slow-growing ennui that resembles mourning, a sense that something or someone has died but you don't know what or who.

It took me a long time to even understand that something unparalleled was happening, that this wasn't going to pass but instead was going to thicken with darkening confusion. Nothing made sense. As I stood helplessly by, my world began to fall apart piece by piece, like a flower whose petals drop one by one as winter approaches.

At first, I resisted. I am adaptable, I am used to solving problems, finding workable solutions, making my way. But none of my usually successful strategies worked. In fact, they seemed to make matters worse. The harder I tried, the faster the breakdowns came. To further confound things, there were periods where I found enough temporary happiness in nature, music, meditation, and relationships to make me think maybe, just maybe, it wasn't so bad after all and I was back to my old self. Then something—it didn't need to be much—would plunge me back into the night and a worsening obscurity.

These cycles went on and on, the darkness edging out the light, until one day I realized that I was the one who was dying, I was the one I was grieving, I knew and controlled nothing. Like being suspended in midair between two trapezes, I stretched out my arms in surrender to what wanted to happen.

That was the turning point in my dark night. I gave up. The person I had been essentially died. There was no longer any point in fighting to get back to normal. The struggle was over. I simply waited for whatever would come, not knowing what shape it would take or what new self would emerge.

It turned out that the waiting allowed the hidden parts of myself to arise, the shadows I had kept in the dark and had not claimed as my own. I had to deal with these arisings one by one. Some were quite familiar, others shocking. Most of all, I realized I had discarded a core part of my true self that I needed to recover and bring into balance. There were other gifts among these reckonings. I found that forgiveness of others and myself freed me from my own imprisonment. Acknowledging my weaknesses gave me new strength. Compassion connected me close up.

This inner working took a long time for me, although I suspect that this was mostly because I repeatedly sought to adapt my old story rather than writing a new one. Finally, a time came when I had the courage to step out into the world to raise a trial balloon. This first step may not have been the right move, but it didn't matter. I was on my way, slowly, slowly, feeling my way into the light. There were a number of setbacks, when I realized I needed to return to the depths to confront yet another demon I hadn't recognized yet. And on it went until I found myself awakening with an arising spaciousness of perspective, a beginning understanding of the transformation I had been through. I gradually painted my new self into existence with the discernment of my expanded awareness. The fog lifted, the mist rose, and there was a new clarity, brilliance, beauty in everything. It was a new dawn.

Five years later, I am again a happy person. I can't say happier, just different. I have a feeling of being more authentically who I am, more whole, a sense there is more light shining through me, that the dark journey I have been on brought the precious gift of greater consciousness. I am more deeply grateful, humbler, and more committed to service. And I am more attuned to the exquisite complexity and connectedness among all things, large and small.

As I reflect on my experience, I am struck by its mythical elements, as I understand myths to be ageless tales told and retold with the same basic patterns to act as a compass for taking needed action in our lives. Dark night stories are these kinds of archetypal myths, tales of descent, transformation and ascent, the darkness holding the gift of sight. These stories are always a quest. There is something missing that through a long road of trials, we come to see is some aspect of ourselves we have discarded and must reclaim, integrating the disowned part into a whole cloth to re-emerge as mature members of society. In our current moment, one of society's most needed quests is the dark night journey to reclaim our lost feminine qualities, in males and females alike, the imbalance in our culture that leaves us feeling disconnected from the world, each other, and ultimately ourselves. The dark night journeys related in the following pages are a retelling of these ancient quests according to the drama of our times and the need for leadership in moving through the dark night of our world.

Introduction

In the midst of winter, I found there was, within me, an
invincible summer.
. . . Albert Camus

In North American culture we are addicted to the
light, to perfection, to material reward. It is often not until
our forties and beyond that the satisfaction we feel from our
worldly achievements begins to wane and is replaced with a
disquiet we often can't quite name. Our psyche, or soul if
you prefer, begins to call to us from the depths, yearning for
balance, for harmony with the powerful ego that has
essentially run the show.

A dark night is the process of finding a new
equilibrium through an inner journey of discovery about
who we really are, retrieving the abandoned parts of our
psyche we have discarded because our culture has told us
they are unacceptable. By bringing them into consciousness,
we regain our sense of being at home in ourselves and our
world. These shadow aspects are seen as "others", that is
other than who we are, and these strangers must be
reclaimed to restore the balance of opposites in our
personality—the shadow as well as ego, the feminine as well
as masculine, the unconscious as well as conscious, in each
of us.

Through negotiating the harrowing dark night journey, we are reborn in a larger container, an expanded Self in which the opposing elements of our psyche reside more harmoniously. Wholeness is the quest of the dark night.

This book is for women and men who are at this kind of a turning point in their personal or professional lives, perhaps feeling bewildered or adrift, that something is missing. What does it mean for us to lose interest in a career to which we have dedicated ourselves or to be forced to leave it for an uncertain future? How does it feel to make the transition into a different kind of work, or no work at all? What do we do after a life-changing illness or accident? Or when a partner leaves or dies? Or when we simply feel alienated from our life, soul-sick and confused? Why are these transitions often a dark night, and how do we understand and navigate the passage?

My hope is to shed light on these questions. I also hope that the transitional experiences described here will be helpful to friends, family, partners and colleagues of those going through a dark night. They may recognize the signs before the affected individual, who may appear to have colloquially "left the building." Dark nights implicate not only the individuals involved but everyone around them. In fact, it is not unusual in the case of sudden illness or accident for loved ones of those in the darkness to be thrown into a dark night of their own.

The book is divided into three parts, each including two chapters. PART ONE, Mapping the Terrain, focuses on the conceptual ideas and the cognitive naming and framing of the dark night, examining its cultural and mythical underpinnings. It introduces the dark night transition as endemic to our Western culture now, as we are called to turn inward, to harmonize the imbalanced poles in our psyche. It describes the characteristics of dark nights and their evolution, as well as addressing several practical questions. It also outlines the particular contribution we can make to the dark night of the world.

In PART TWO, The Many Ways We Travel, the perspective shifts to real-life examples of what dark nights look like, beginning with a comprehensive description of my own dark night story, expanded with journal entries, dreams, reflections and learnings. The dark night stories of two men and four women follow, with their experiences arrayed across the stages of the journey, giving a clear picture of both the commonalities and the distinctions of the passage at each stage.

In PART THREE, the conceptual and experiential perspectives are woven together through a dozen of the most common themes in dark nights. Guidance for navigating each phase in the transition is charted.

The conclusion returns the call to you, the reader, to undertake your own dark night passage to wholeness for the sake of the whole world. Finally, an Appendix offers a deeper look at the dark feminine myths that illustrate the transformation.

I hope that by sharing this analysis of dark night stories, I can aid those like me who find themselves in the mystery of this baffling terrain. I hope that readers in the midst of a true dark night will feel my empathy for your losses and challenges and take heart that you are not alone. If you find yourself a little unsettled but not yet feeling like you're wandering in the desert, then this book will provide helpful guidance for what is to come. If you've been stuck in inertia, then perhaps reading what follows will support your movement toward resolution or give you some sense of companionship. And if you are emerging into the light on the far side of a dark night experience, you may find the ways of integration helpful in bringing yourself into wholeness.

PART ONE:

MAPPING THE TERRAIN

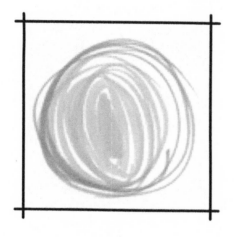

Chapter One
Dark Night of the Self

In the dark times, will there also be singing?
Yes, there will also be singing, about the dark times.
. . . Bertolt Brecht

What is a Dark Night?

There are several major transitions throughout our lives. As we move from childhood to adulthood through our teens, we go through tumultuous shifts in identity and independence. As adults, our first dark night—perhaps we should call it our dark dusk—usually comes in our forties, where we have what has often been called a midlife crisis. Sometimes it is forced upon us by circumstances. Other times we can be driven to change by restlessness or dissatisfaction. This transition usually focuses on our external conditions. We change careers, end a relationship, buy a new car, take a long trip, or have a fling. Although these changes bubble up from the inside, we look outward into our world for the means to accomplish the adjustments we seek. The process is, in essence, a recognition that youth has ended and maturity is ahead of us.

While it can be a hair-raising time, we mostly manage to get over it and get on with life for a decade or two until a deeper dark night emerges, one that may change who we fundamentally are: our beliefs, values, and perspectives. And if my experience is any indication, this dark night is perhaps the deepest of the transitions we will make, often the longest and most difficult to accomplish because it forces us to question everything we thought true. What we find is that our lifelong reliance on the external world has, over time, resulted in a correspondingly ragged and threadbare under layer. The leanness of the self within is a reality for many of us.

This more profound dark night requires a turning inward to confront our deepest illusions, those abandoned parts of ourselves we may not even be aware of, or truths we have not wanted to confront. We contemplate our lives so far and how we want to spend the time remaining to us as the creeping sense of our own mortality grows. We may encounter death in a serious way for the first time as we begin to suffer losses. We may feel the need to recreate ourselves from the inside out, upsetting our most preciously held principles. If our earlier dark dusk was finding ourselves, this deeper dark night is losing ourselves, requiring that we rebuild our sense of who we are from the ground up.

Ironically, the more successful we have been in overcoming the outer challenges in our lives, the darker these nights seem to be. In a proverbial failure of success, we tend to be more attached to our accomplishments and less likely to let them go easily. We hold on to what we know. It is often the feminine aspects of ourselves *in here* we have ignored in order to make our way *out there* in the masculine world. Our first instinct is to resist, drive on, to keep doing what we've always done in the hope that something different will happen, while in fact the crisis deepens. The surrender required paradoxically feels like a failure when in fact it is the only route through the confusion. It requires *being* in our world of *doing*.

Awareness of these passages has been growing along with our developing consciousness for hundreds of years. In the thirteenth century, Dante Alighieri in his *Divine Comedy* described finding himself in a dark wood that was "wild, harsh and impenetrable." Three centuries later, St. John of the Cross, a Jesuit priest, wrote of his *Dark Night of the Soul*, about "an obscure and dark and terrible purgation." They were both speaking of a relinquishing of the ego, acknowledging the shadows and imperfections of the person's life in order to create deeper meaning and purpose. These early reflections represent a first documenting of the inner struggle associated with a change in worldview, an expansion of consciousness about the nature of reality and one's self.

In St. John's time, the late 1500s, the soul simply meant the personality in its striving for something beyond the egoic self. The dark night was a dis-identifying with the personality in order to see more clearly the divine true nature of the person. In today's secular Western world, these transition processes have escaped the cloisters and been recognized as normal passages in the development of adult consciousness. We may not associate our own divinity with consciousness development and yet the dark night and its themes are alive and well today, drawing us through the transformation into more inclusive, expansive, interconnected and whole human beings.

Author and mystic Caroline Myss says, "Mystics without monasteries come from every walk of life, from every spiritual tradition, and from no spiritual tradition."[1] As we live longer and are more self-aware, we become mystics without monasteries, discovering our unique path toward wholeness.

Integral philosopher Ken Wilber writes about dark nights in his theories of development in individuals and cultures. He describes them as transitions between our evolutionary stages of development, what he refers to as our consciousness "waking up." In *Integral Spirituality*, he says they represent "a passing through, or a letting go, of attachment or addiction to a particular reality."[2] We are essentially stripped of our identity in order to take on new ideas and interests. As we mature in our outlook through the stages of adulthood, we take on broader perspectives and are able to see many more sides to the story. Each time we pass through one of these changes in worldview, we take on new values and expanded ways of understanding and enacting them. We see the world in a different light and create new meaning from our experiences.

Harvard psychologist Robert Kegan says we are essentially meaning-making systems. The way we make meaning of the events of our lives gives rise to our sense of self, of who we are. The elements of the psyche that make up our personality operate in the space between an external event and our reaction to it. In this between-space, we create the meaning that makes sense of our world and ourselves in it. This self is a mediator and meaning-maker, continuously evolving and adapting within the life structure we have built from our choices.

Because we tend to prefer certainty and stability, we make the gradual changes in our understandings fit the current life structure until the gap gets so large that we can no longer ignore the dissonance. It is then that we get the call to adventure, the psyche's demand for balance with the ego, requiring us to enter a wasteland where we must reinvent the meaning-making system that gives rise to a new Self. This is the dark night process.

Dark nights are a surrendering of our attachment to the identities we hold most dear so we can take on a more expansive mental model of ourselves and the world. They are accompanied by the suffering and loss that this surrendering entails. These boundary passages can happen without our paying much attention, but they are more often accompanied by an upset, a disjuncture in our lives where we feel the loss of who we were at the same time as we are paradoxically becoming more conscious, more awake to the reality of who we actually are. In her book *Necessary Losses,* Judith Viorst beautifully names these passages in the subtitle, saying they are "The Loves, illusions, dependencies and impossible expectations that all of us have to give up in order to grow." She begins in childhood, where we have to give up our belief in Santa Claus, for example, and continues through adulthood with the increasing difficulty of the losses associated with aging and death.

As we become more conscious of our consciousness, we can step back to consider these transitions as natural progressions that we can learn about and learn from. While each major change experience will be unique to our individual character and the circumstances of our lives, we can look for underlying patterns to guide us through what is a disorienting, unsettled time.

A Map of the Dark Night Process

Despite the uniqueness of each individual's life unfolding, there is a similar transformational process to these dark night journeys. They are a natural occurrence and have been happening since we became conscious of our own evolutionary story. In 1949, Joseph Campbell coined the term "hero's journey" after studying the most compelling myths and stories told across many time periods and cultures. The key elements of these stories are consistent, forming the substrate of our most cherished tales of love, war and change, from *The Mists of Avalon* to the *Star Wars* adventures. They are stories of waking up and growing up. Campbell called this story behind all stories the "monomyth."

However, while the hero's journey presents a compelling framework, it has been criticized for being a rather masculine interpretation, calling on the masculine aspects in each of us—whether male or female—as the story is told, one of dragons, conquests, heroics and trophies.

If the hero's journey is the warp of the story, what is the weft? Because the dark night is a journey toward wholeness, an integration of the masculine and the feminine in each of us, it is therefore important to also highlight the lesser-known feminine aspects of the transformation process. What new information or perspective might the feminine mythologies offer? How might a combined account be woven together, including not only the more comfortable masculine-oriented perspective but also the less developed feminine side? What might we learn from a unified point of view?

The story behind the feminine mythologies has been underplayed in our patriarchal culture for several hundred years.

The power of these mythical stories is that they are so recognizable. They have been countless times in the ancient journey to the dark goddess, the dark feminine, in different cultures throughout history. She is Kali, Cerridwyn, Persephone, Medusa, and Hecate. In hundreds of fairy tales she plays the witch, the wicked stepmother, or the evil queen. She is represented in nature's cycles, the dark phases of the moon and the fallow seasons of the year. She is embodied in the Black Madonnas, who are worshipped all over the world, and acknowledged by the growing numbers of followers of Mary Magdalene. And she is also in the psyche, in the unknown parts of ourselves, the underworld of our personalities held in darkness, out of consciousness.

The feminine represents a shadow side of our psyche, the opposite pole that needs to be reclaimed as part of our dark night discovery. For women of our "animus-obsessed" generation, the re-emergence of the feminine, especially the dark feminine that lives beneath our conscious awareness, holds a powerful place in our dark night journeys to become whole, unified, graceful adults. And men are often in need of this same kind of integration of both the light and dark feminine on their way to wholeness.

What I am proposing, then, is a "duomyth" story of the dark night, a journey made up of both the his-tories and her-stories of mythology, portrayed as a cycle of descent, transition and ascent, a death of the current self and rebirth into a larger consciousness.

The model below outlines the three-part process through the dark night, indicating the major phases encountered along the way. However, it should not be taken as a sequential step-wise process. There may be many cycles within this overall journey, wheels within wheels of descent and ascent as the exploration continues.

A dark night begins when we feel out of place, uneasy in our own skin, called to something different we can't identify. There is an invitation, a persistent call from the psyche that draws us forward. But there are costs to the adventurous path, so we try to ignore the call or answer it with a whisper. Despite our initial resistance, it doesn't go away. Eventually, we are drawn to act upon our dis-ease and enter into the darkness, committing to a path of change. We step into the journey not knowing where we are headed or even why.

We descend down into the earth, the underworld, as we are stripped of our attachments and exposed, surrendering our most precious beliefs, self-images, behaviour or defenses, anything we cling to that prevents us from completing the descent. Our identities crumble and we don't recognize ourselves. Nothing may seem to work anymore. We come apart and can't be put back together again.

It is through this process of dissolution that we are able to see clearly, perhaps for the first time, the Discarded Other at the core of our psyche, the previously unconscious part of ourselves we have abandoned or rejected. There in the darkness, we die to our current selves. At the lowest point, the darkness can be all-consuming as we become passive and reflective. We grieve. We wait.

Our time of mourning our losses in the underworld can be short or long. It is a mysterious time without rules. We can get stuck in the depths, caught in the between-space without the energy or direction to begin the ascent. This sense of powerlessness is a languor that may look like depression but may instead be a kind of absence of presence, a going to ground, a winter, a dead zone where we are barely inhabiting our days, watching them from a place apart. This mourning in the underworld darkens everything in our surroundings. Things do not go on as before but are left untended.

Often, a guide will invite us to consider something that becomes the seed of our rebirth. After a germination time in the dark earth, there is a sense of expectancy, of pregnancy, of birthing something new. We feel new life growing and begin the ascent, accumulating our new personality and worldview in reverse of the shedding of the descent. The climb may be slow and have additional setbacks and challenges requiring patience and compassion as we rebuild and embody our new lives, integrating our learning from the journey.

After a period of rest, we return to our familiar places and see them as if for the first time. The dawn has come. We slowly begin to take our new energy and identity out into the world and share the gifts of light we have been given.

Practical Questions

The foregoing tells us about dark nights, their history and character, but it doesn't tell us much about the practicalities of being in one. We are full of questions as the darkness invades our lives, and these questions tend to revolve around basic concerns.

When I found myself entering this foreign territory, what I really wanted was someone to sit me down and answer my very practical questions. Like what brings on a dark night, how do you know you are in one, and how long do they last? I went in search of guidance and support for working through my confusion. At the risk of generalizing what are unique experiences, I provide here my current understanding about these practical concerns.

What causes dark nights to occur?

There are many catalysts to dark night journeys. Some come from the circumstances of our lives: the loss of a job, a loved one, or our health. In these cases, we may feel thrown into disorientation and confusion, made keenly aware of our lack of choice and control. We may feel immobilized, bewildered or angry. The lives we have known are gone, along with their meaning and purpose.

Other dark nights seem to come along with natural changes in life stages as we age, such as reduced work activity or moving into retirement, dealing with an empty nest as children grow up and away, or stepping back from community involvement. It may also be that things just get to be too much: multitasking doesn't work as well, business travel isn't as much fun, or being constantly busy just feels tiring. These conditions may trigger a slower slide into a dark night and be harder to identify as catalysts but will bring the same growing sense of ennui and loss of meaning that darkens over time. Our friends and family members may wonder where we've gone, whether we're depressed, what they can do.

Dark nights may also be brought about through our own inner workings. We may have to come to terms with our own limitations: the expectations of our youth won't be fulfilled, we have missed opportunities that won't come again, we are not the people we had hoped to be. We may spend increasing amounts of time in reflection and perhaps take to heart feedback we've been given and ignored. We begin to realize that our time ahead may be less than what has already been and become more aware of our mortality. This life review process is common as we move through our adulthood but if we take it seriously, it may expose many of the delusions we have mistakenly held about ourselves, requiring a wholesale rethinking of our values, life choices, and purpose.

How do we know we are in a dark night?

We might not know we are in a dark night until we are quite deep into the process. Even if we experience an unexpected loss that throws us into turmoil, we might not realize that we are at the beginning of creating a whole new identity. We might believe we can mourn this loss like others we have suffered, where we just plowed our way through it or plowed it under to be dealt with at a later time, leaning into our addictions to cover up our grief, confusion and uncertainty.

We tend to cling to our usual worldviews despite mounting evidence the picture no longer fits. In this wandering phase, everything is so confusing that although we can feel a mist rolling in, we can also turn and look back to the outlines of our familiar life. Despite the unrelenting call to venture forward, we may still feel the pull to return to our old patterns and step haltingly over the threshold into the passage. We will probably not have a language to adequately describe our experience even to ourselves, let alone others. We are committing to a journey of some kind, but it is so amorphous that we may wonder if it isn't just a temporary murky bivouac before the sun shines again and we move on with our usual habits and habitats.

These cycles can repeat for months, even years, before we fully realize there is no going back—we really have crossed into new territory where, if we want to continue to grow as a person, we must relinquish our most valued attachments, addictions and emotional bonds. When we have trouble recognizing our former selves, when we feel naked and raw, stumbling and bereft, then we know without question we are in the darkness of a deep night. Then the work begins.

It is important to note that dark nights can be quite depressing and, at their deepest and most volatile stages, can descend into clinical depression for a time. At its darkest points, the force of physical and emotional upheaval could require medical intervention. Most psychiatrists today see depression as a continuum of severity from normal sadness to extreme melancholy, with no clear qualitative boundary between what is and is not mental illness. Diagnosis depends on the context: the capacity to respond appropriately to life events, the degree of functional impairment, the duration and intensity of symptoms. Dark nights may exist all along the continuum. At the blackest moments in the process, it may be that treatment is necessary for a time and it is critical to seek help if debilitation and isolation persist or thoughts of suicide are present. In fact, it is most helpful in any case to have a therapist or counsellor who can walk alongside us, support our grieving, normalize our experience, and recommend further medical referral if necessary.

Mostly, though, we are able to inhabit our days, although perhaps at half-speed or less and without much joy. Grief and mourning are central characteristics of the losses we endure, accompanied by mild depression. However, just as there is an insistent call to adventure at the outset of the process, there is also the faint but adamant call to rebirth at our darkest hour.

How long do dark nights last?

Well, as they say, that depends. The short answer is they are rarely measured in months and commonly last years. The real work of the dark night—the confronting of our shadows and delusions—can begin in earnest only when we are able to admit we are in one. This initial phase can itself take years to accomplish. It lasts as long as we resist and deny the call from the unknown. Those of us who have high self-efficacy are especially susceptible because we are used to exercising some measure of control over our circumstances. This tendency can extend the time it takes to fully engage the process as we struggle to hold onto our customary ways of being in the world.

Once we acknowledge that something unprecedented is taking place, then the length of the process depends on our willingness to lean into our own brokenness, to face our deepest fears, longings and loathings, and to accept these shadows as part of who we are, to surface them and identify with them. Because this work is arduous, we tend to accomplish it a little at a time, pausing to digest the naked truths about our characters, our choices, and our regrets. We can be distracted, drawn back to our past pursuits in an effort to escape the darkness. Sometimes this is a necessary respite, but it usually ends in dissatisfaction as we are pulled back into the night to complete the work we are meant to do.

There are temporary times of joy, laughter, connection and contribution. As our new identity takes shape, these moments multiply. We begin to feel more graceful, more grateful. There is a new sense of belonging in our bodies and minds at this time, of rightness with the world. We see the gift of new consciousness we've been given and appreciate the spaciousness and simplicity that come with it. We make the slow ascent, incorporating the work of the dark night into our expanded awareness of who we are. There are many more gifts in this phase and if we are in too much haste, we miss them. This is a part of the journey to be unhurriedly savoured as we rebuild our new selves, revelling in the mystery of how it has all happened and wondering what we might make of our new connections back out in the world.

The value of becoming self-aware about dark nights is that they can then be more easily recognized and negotiated. Although they're still not easy, we can understand the cycle for ourselves and also support our loved ones through the adventure. Further, if we can become familiar with the process, befriend the darkness and see it as creating a harmonious relationship between the opposing poles in our psyche, we can perhaps engage it as an ongoing process in smaller steps rather than a complete overhaul. We can more easily recognize our familiar patterns and engage in self-exploration and renewal. Finally, we can understand that the darkness is always with us. It, too, is part of who we are.

[1] Myss, Carolyn. *Entering the Castle: Finding the inner path to god and your soul's purpose* (New York: Atria, 2007), 33.

[2] Wilber, Ken. *Integral Spirituality: A startling new role for religion in the modern and postmodern world* (Boulder CO: Shambala, 2007), 99.

Chapter Two
Dark Night of the World

To go in the dark with a light is to
know the light.
To know the dark, go dark.
. . . Wendell Berry

Now that we have an idea of what a dark night looks like at the individual level, we can take a giant step back in perspective to see the larger purpose for making the journey. It is not only to heal what has been abandoned within us or to broaden our consciousness about our own reality. It is also to develop the capacity to influence the world's dark night journey to greater wholeness as well. For it is through our individual dark nights that we come to a place where we can see the collective issues facing us more clearly and respond with the necessary awareness and compassion.

As the saying goes: as within, so without. Individual and collective are inextricably intertwined. The evolution of humanity as a whole, too, has proceeded through this dance of opposites, rebalancing from stage to stage in civilization through a process of transformation both within and without. Major epochal developments—the shifts from tribal foraging to agriculture, then to industrial nations and now to global interconnectedness—have all involved major upheavals and transformations in our worldviews, transcending yet including all that has come before.

Einstein is famous for saying that we can't solve today's problems with the same level of consciousness that created them. Our problems tend to get ahead of us because we prefer the status quo, adapting to our current circumstances rather than entering into a major change. Just as with individuals, our larger systems eventually reach a stage where they are no longer sustainable. We either change or are changed by them. This is the societal call to enter the darkness and find the Discarded Other that awaits in the shadows to be reclaimed, a new equilibrium for the future of humanity.

Many people believe we are at such a stage today, facing irreversible choices as a planet. We see the signs of breakdown all around us—the poverty and degradation, the injustice and greed—yet we are puzzled about how to make a meaningful difference. We resist the upheaval in our lifestyles that will be required. We mourn the loss of planetary biodiversity, of a moral compass, and worry about the lives of our unborn children. As we confront these shadows in our culture, we may see that the Discarded Other at this level is not very different from our own Discarded Other, just at a much bigger scale.

Our current worn out patriarchy needs to be renewed with an expansive consciousness of global care and concern emanating from a place of inclusive, equitable and ethical values. This place emerges from the integrated Self. It is as much about who we are as it is about what we do. It is an inside job!

The question for us, then, is how we as maturing adults at this point in history can collectively contribute to a new planetary wholeness. What role can we play in contributing to the worldwide crisis confronting us now? I believe we are entering a period where with our extended lifespan, health and prosperity, we can play a unique leadership role in alleviating suffering and creating the conditions for humanity's surviving and thriving.

When the twentieth century began, life expectancy at birth in North America was less than fifty years. We are now expected to live into our eighties, and this raises new possibilities for continuing contribution, about who we might be and how we might apply ourselves over the thirty years or more we have in front of us.

The naysayers would have us believe the aging population is going to cause tremendous economic hardship for the fewer younger workers who will have to finance our declining years as we drain the public coffers with our healthcare costs. Many of them view the generation retiring over the next couple of decades as a social burden, waiting in a long line for the grim reaper to relieve us from our endless games of golf and early bird dinners on the social purse. There is no doubt that some of us will succumb to health issues, need extensive care, and take out of the treasury more than we put in. But many others of us will have the energy, the time and means, the experience and desire to be of service that suggests a very different future.

We may in fact be the largest population cohort in human history to be afforded the opportunity for nonviolent involvement at a critical threshold of major change. There are estimated to be about seventy million baby boomers in North America leaving the workforce over the next twenty years. That amounts to about ten thousand people *per day* becoming available to create a different world. We have made it up to suit ourselves all the way along. We must not stop now.

However, our ability to contribute for the next thirty years depends on our *not* behaving in the same ways we've behaved for the last thirty years. We need a combination of the masculine strengths we have overdeveloped and the feminine values we have underplayed, a coming into alignment now that our choices no longer revolve around our youthful obligations and imperatives. Facing our mortality and dealing with loss, reclaiming the discarded parts of ourselves, moving beyond ego, not knowing the answers or even the questions—these are capacities we need to develop to become the leaders and the social healers that the world needs now.

We have more wealth, resources, longevity, wisdom and influence than ever before. In fact, we could say we have an accountability to repair some of the excesses of our youth and their consequences, to pioneer a simpler, more sustainable path for the sake of our planet and our great grandchildren.

Whoever we have been in our careers, our core competencies are different as we move into this stage of leadership. These competencies include all of our hard-earned capacities but transcend them for the sake of the whole rather than the part to which we have been connected in our earlier lives. Where we have competed, we are now called to collaborate. Where we have sought individual gain, we are now called to collective development. Where we have identified with our professional disciplines, we are now called to interdisciplinary integration. And where we have focused on our families, communities and countries, we are now called to see the whole world as our home.

We have the freedom and responsibility to discover the next evolutionary unfolding of what it means to be wholly human, laying down new tracks into the future, packing with us the strengths of our experience and adding to it an expansive new awareness as seasoned sages leading from our whole selves on behalf of the whole world.

There are many books and articles being written about shaping the political and social agenda for the coming decades. The purpose here is to outline a transformation process that will prepare us to take on these socio-political tasks with the necessary care and concern that only a deep self-awareness and wisdom can bring to the dark night that our world is now facing. It is not that each of us has to contribute at a large scale, but we must be able to see into the broad issues that confront us with the empathy of our own seasoned experience and the intimacy of our own unified psyches. Then we can begin where we are, bringing our singular perspectives to the world in whatever ways are available to us. We can become those the world needs us to be.

PART TWO:

THE MANY WAYS WE TRAVEL

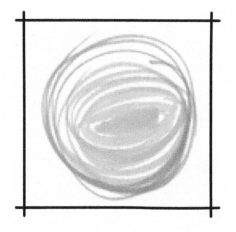

Chapter Three
My Dark Night Story

Guided by my heritage of a love of beauty and a respect for
strength—in search of my mother's garden, I found my own.
. . . Alice Walker

I am a woman entering my seventh decade, having
lived all of my years in North America, although I've
travelled extensively throughout the world. I have been
interested in leadership since my early thirties, when I was
given responsibility to supervise a colleague, to provide
leadership, and I realized I had no idea what that meant.
Nowhere in my training as a workplace designer had the
word "leader" even been mentioned. I returned to school to
do a master's degree in organization development, where I
learned that leadership is all about change.

The eighties were heady days when we believed we
were in the midst of a paradigm shift that would improve the
quality of working life for employees. However, senior
leaders were rarely part of our interventions, so the
outcomes were partial. Leadership remained a mystery to
me despite leading groups dedicated to its development.
Back to school I went, this time to complete doctoral work
on leadership in turbulent times, searching for leadership
competencies suitable for rapid change, complexity and

uncertainty, the hallmarks of organizational environments in the nineties.

My work over the next decade allowed me to apply my knowledge at more and more senior corporate levels, to set vision and strategy for the future and lead broader organizational change processes. I taught postgraduate leadership courses to share my experience and pass along the insights I had gained. In the end, though, I found myself burnt out and disillusioned, a failure in achieving the promise of a new world of work through change-oriented leadership.

Entering my fifties, I attended a coach training program and began to turn to leadership at the individual and small-team levels with organizational cultures only in the background. Coaching, I learned, is about personal change, leading from the inside out, from self-awareness and mutual trust. This shift in focus had two major influences. It brought me up close to the leaders I was coaching and teaching, allowing me to see into their challenges and support their personal growth. It also required that I look into myself as a leader, to turn inward to learn about my own shadows and limitations, and to concentrate on my self-development as a whole person.

For fifteen years I grew as a leader coach, leading through coaching and coaching through leading a consultancy working with leaders around the world. With my colleagues, I taught hundreds of business and community leaders to be coaches. I wrote and spoke about this style of *Leadership Alchemy* to create inside-out leaders in cultures of meaning and contribution.

Five years ago, it was time to ease up a little—to rest on my laurels, work part-time, enjoy life. But that was not what was in store. Instead, I did a deep dive into darkness, making all my previous challenges pale by comparison.

My story is an example of one of the dark night journeys described in Part One. It is an interpretation of my experience looking back with some distance from the actual events. To give a flavour of my feelings in the moments I am recounting, I have included examples of my dreams, poetry, and journal entries. Writing from my current reality beyond the dark night story I am telling, I feel more complete than I felt while experiencing it. I couldn't tell this story when I was in it. I was engulfed in it, unable to see through the dark enough to even believe there would be an end to it. From where I am now I can be more objective because I can see the arc of the whole story, or at least the story so far.

The dark night map presented in Chapter Two is shown below, adapted to more specifically describe my particular experience, again in three parts: the Descent, the Underworld, and the Ascent.

The Descent

The Call: The Loss of Feeling at Home

I remember thinking I was done with Toronto. I had lived there for forty years. My executive coaching business had become rote, the international travel was exhausting, the city was increasingly congested, and my house didn't feel like home. I was restless for something different—I wasn't sure what, but the itch was persistent.

A few years earlier, I had bought a house on the Gatineau River in Chelsea, Quebec, where my father and his family had spent summers. I had rented it out with the idea that I would retire there, and this seemed to me the perfect answer to my agitation as I approached my sixty-fifth birthday. It was time to step back from my intense pace of work and bustling city life. There was some appeal in the rolling green countryside, my ancestry there, some friends and relatives, a large house with a garden on the river, and hopefully a place of peace and belonging. As a former interior designer, I looked forward to turning the house into a cozy home where my husband and I could spend summers as we aged. I had a clear vision of myself standing with my arms wide open in the front yard, welcoming family and friends into our beautiful space.

We left Toronto in June and moved excitedly into the Chelsea house. I was completely unprepared for the way the summer unfolded. I expected it to be a new beginning—a new home, a new neighbourhood, a renewed connection with my father's family, with just enough work in nearby Ottawa to keep me from getting bored. Instead, it was full of conflict with my husband about how we would live, how we would deal with the house, and how we would spend our time. Very early on, we had an offer from a neighbour who knew the house and wanted to buy it. In my heart I already suspected it wasn't the place for us, but selling meant a quick decision and having to leave mid-summer, much earlier than we had planned. I thought we should sell but allowed myself to be persuaded that it was too quick and we should continue with the upgrades and sell in the fall, if that was what we decided.

Through the summer, we spent our time arguing over the specifics of the needed renovations and making endless trips to the hardware store. I worked diligently with our contractor, all the while hating myself for not standing my ground. I resented having to complete the renovation when we could have sold. I was on my own quite a bit as my husband continued to travel for work. I struggled with the growing sense of losing myself—losing focus, meaning, direction and energy for anything but tiles, paint, and cabinets. I was a bit like an automaton, moving through the days but not entirely there. I couldn't engage with my coaching work to any extent, either; it was just more of the same. And my connections with family and friends were unable to boost my enthusiasm for long.

The more this malaise gathered around me, the harder I fought to keep it at bay. I was possessed with getting everything right but the more I tried, the more things felt wrong. The renovation was beautiful but it didn't feel like home. It was too remote for me as a city dweller and I didn't feel I belonged after all. I remember taking pictures of each of the rooms—they looked so inviting, right out of a magazine—but I wasn't in them and they didn't feel as if they were intended for me. I was confused and perplexed. I wrote in my journal, "I've been feeling depressed the past few days—doubts, disappointments, dilemmas . . . I've lost my sense of play."

In the end, I sold the Chelsea house for the same price we could have had in June before any of the renovations. I gave away over half of my furniture, books, and other belongings, and piled the remainder into a shipping container left in the driveway. We even said goodbye to the resident mouse we called Hector, who appeared in the middle of the dining room on one of our final mornings, dead with his feet in the air. With a sad sigh of relief, I headed south to my husband's home for the winter.

In retrospect, I had probably been experiencing a sense of ennui for at least a couple of years, but I was so used to driving on, pushing through, that I didn't pay much attention. It was simply another rough spot to manage. I had been on a fast track education and career trajectory for about forty years, at a time when opportunities were plentiful and women were especially encouraged to compete.

The catalyst for this rocket launch had been the sudden death of my mother in my early twenties. She was the archetype of the feminine: beautiful, flowing, artistic, at the center of everything. She was full of life and ideas. Her friends called her a bohemian, *Auntie Mame,* after the movie with Rosalind Russell whom she resembled with her dark Poodle Cut hair. I had followed along in her wake as the only daughter, being creative, flighty, and unmotivated. We had a difficult relationship through my early years, and it was only after I left home at nineteen that we were able to begin to develop a closer bond. Then suddenly, she was gone. Her death was profoundly shocking to me, incomprehensible. My immature and unconscious response was to reject the feminine in me out of fear that I would suffer the same fate. Instead I chose to follow the masculine path and to do so with a vengeance. My father had always been happy despite a life full of losses and hardships. It appeared a much better choice.

But now, four decades later, I was tired, finding it more and more difficult to summon the energy for the same old game. I realize now that the inner world calling me was the feminine, the cast-off part of myself whose voice was getting too loud to ignore. The only voice I could identify at the time was a lack of feeling at home. This nomadic search for a sense of home had followed me through life, through the many homes I had lived in, made and remade in a relentless effort to feel I belonged. The move to the country house in Chelsea was yet another attempt to answer the call by looking outside myself rather than turning inward to learn how to belong at home in my own skin.

The previous winter I had enrolled in a master's degree program in Integral Theory to give myself a new challenge. It was mostly online and captured my growing interest in consciousness and complexity. I had returned to school successfully many times previously when things were at an impasse. But this time, while the program was stimulating intellectually, it reinforced my flatness and melancholy. I was older than all of the teachers and most of the other students, again leaving me feeling out of place.

To compensate, I put even more energy into my academic classes, my reading and essays, all escapes from my own turmoil. I became very focused on the idea of home as an expression of self and did a good deal of research on it as part of my studies. It seemed a way to connect with what was going on for me, although I was just beginning to link the notion of home with the feminine. I was circling all around the edges of it but resisting the now-obvious connection.

In the spring, needing a Canadian home, I rented a condo in Vancouver, where my son had relocated with his wife and my three-year-old grandson. Another child was on the way and I wanted to be part of their young lives. I settled in and got to know the city, feeling that this was a place I could be happy. I loved the smaller city, my walkable neighbourhood and the friends I met. One of my dearest friends also lived nearby. We had been teaching partners for a couple of decades and had written a book together. She welcomed me and folded me into her life. This was a period of respite that buoyed my spirits and brought me alive again. I wrote in my journal, "I have so loved being here, living here, the whole adventure of it, the discovery of this wonderful city, exploring its delights. I didn't realize how far I had drifted from a sense of family, of belonging by birth, or how much I missed it."

At about this time, another friend I had known for years asked if I would be interested in partnering with him to create workshops on developing our consciousness. We gathered a community of fellow explorers around us and facilitated several successful four-day workshops. They were a salvation, an opportunity for me to turn inward in the company of others and look at my own evolution and development. I was suddenly energized and keen to explore this new inner territory. I was coming to the end of the Integral Theory program and looking for a window into my growing understanding of the transition I was in. The opportunity to work with a community of kindred spirits exploring this mysterious terrain of inner consciousness felt like just what I needed. I was becoming more intensely aware that some major change was pushing in at the edges of my awareness, but the life my husband and I had created was so comfortable that I was able to ignore the assembling storm clouds.

Into the Darkness: Confusion, Breakdown, Questioning

Over the next year, things began to fall apart all around me. I kept trying to find the way out, the thing that would bring me back to normal. I had been through major transitions before and had managed them using several successful strategies. My intellect, courage and a steely resolve together had allowed me to feel confident in taking the risks necessary to see me through the hard times. However, these strategies, so effective in the external masculine world, proved not only fruitless but worsened my situation in the internal world I was entering.

My husband's southern home where I spent half the year became less and less a place of peace. The house we had lived in for fifteen years was desperate for a kitchen renovation and again, I plunged into creating a harmonious space that instead pulled my relationship apart as it came together, a beautiful place where I didn't belong and was increasingly unhappy. What began as a minor upgrade kept expanding. We not only redesigned the entire kitchen and laundry area, but also included both bathrooms and the wet bar, put in a new hardwood floor, and repainted the entire house while we were at it. I found myself spending even more time on my own, my husband travelling so he wouldn't have to be involved in the renovation or the consequent conflict between us. My coaching work had dried up and my academic program was complete. I spent the winter with the house torn apart all around me, mirroring the way I felt on the inside. My journal says it all.

> *I will just say this much. I am in trouble, in my life, with my choices and dilemmas. I have been avoiding it, hoping it was a passing phase, but it occupies more of my time and affects my behaviour. To say it aloud, even in writing and only to myself, makes it more real, more true. I shall sit with the knowledge spoken for a while and see where it leads. This is not a thing to be hurried.*

I was on an emotional roller coaster, drowning in sadness and regret, then feeling tremendous anger, and the next day feeling hopeful and encouraged. It was exhausting!

One of the reprieves from the renovation mess at home was our annual ski week in Utah. We had invited friends to join us in our timeshare condo there and I was enjoying the hills, the speed, the powder. At the top of a lift, I pushed off without realizing that my husband was standing on the back of my left ski. As my right ski went down the hill, my left knee twisted behind me and I sunk to the ground in pain. He said, "I didn't see you." I felt it on so many levels! The result, after a toboggan ride down the hill to the clinic, several doctors and an MRI, was a torn ligament and fragments of bone pulled away from my kneecap.

I returned to Vancouver to see an orthopedic surgeon, who fitted me for an automotive steel brace from my upper thigh to midway down my calf with six straps to secure it, in the hope that I wouldn't need surgery. I then went back to our southern home to complete the renovation. I remember sitting in the living room in a puddle of tears as I struggled to figure out how the unwieldy brace went together with all those numbered straps, wondering how I would ever be able to move in it.

But figure it out I did and, after a few weeks, my husband and I both left for work in Alberta, me with long full skirts covering my brace. No one at the workshop knew I had it on, but I felt ugly and awkward. I remember thinking I was an invalid and playing with in-valid, as it described my sense of self so well. My journal described my sorry state.

I am deeply in despair about us. The chasm is so wide and unassailable I can't imagine how it will ever be crossed. I am about out of forgiveness and generosity for it and just feeling so sad, so disappointed, I don't know what to do. I have given up hope that any meaningful connection is possible. It feels like going through the motions without any authentic joy. What am I to do? I know the answer—I'm just having trouble with the enactment.

I asked my husband for a month in Vancouver on my own to re-center and consider our relationship. I felt physically and emotionally in fragments, like my knee, the pieces of my life scattered around me in disarray. I wasn't sure I could continue in the marriage but wanted to sit with my feelings in stillness to see what emerged. I was questioning everything. I felt like an injured animal crawling back to the lair for comfort and familiarity, for solace and quiet. I meditated, I journaled, I read; I tried to find my best self above the confusion.

One of the sages I learned from during these weeks was mystic healer Caroline Myss. Her book *Entering the Castle* allowed me to expose many of my shadows to the light, to atone in a way for the sins of my past: my pride and arrogance, my judgements and projections, my need for control, the lies I told myself and others to sustain my image of myself. I made long lists of my betrayals, my seductions and temptations, and my selfishness. I wrote, "My need to be best, to be superior, drives my perfectionism. Anything less is just ordinary. I need to prove I am worthy. Underneath, I feel I am out of control, powerless, unworthy of love."

Bathing in this humility, I also realized that I had been given many gifts: my capacity for joy and play, my self-awareness and courage to change, my call to be of service in the world. As the weeks passed, I found myself able to move from blame to forgiveness, from the negative view of what was happening to a more positive, expansive perspective on my blessings and privileges. After all, the damage to my knee was an accident, and my discontent was my problem, not his. At the end of the month, my husband and I negotiated a plan to renew our relationship, including couple's therapy, although I believe we both felt in our depths that it was yet another attempt to put Humpty Dumpty back together again.

That spring, another distraction arose. A local university asked if I would design a coach training program to be offered as a continuing studies certificate. I felt very much at home in universities and thought it might be an outlet for some of my restless muddle. Once more, I dove in with my friend and teaching colleague and we designed and delivered our first program over the next year. It was a monumental effort that required obtaining university senate approval, meeting the complex credentialing requirements of the coaching federation, and gathering the participants and resources necessary for the program.

Working over the next six months, we were successful in the design and approval phases, able to begin the pilot offering of the program that fall. I saw it as a kind of legacy program, incorporating all the learning we had gained in many previous teaching assignments. However, although the students and classes were successful far beyond our expectations, the university administration proved exceedingly frustrating. As the program director I struggled continuously, from the first marketing session through to the end of the pilot program.

The final straw came when the exhaustive online credentialing submission we had prepared was somehow lost by the same program manager who had been my nemesis from the outset. We had worked for two solid weeks to complete the detailed online process the accrediting body required and had already tacitly approved. In tired disillusionment, we again sent the pieces for him to reassemble and submit. We were subsequently told by email that we wouldn't be asked back and that our submission had failed to achieve the highest level of accreditation. We were not given any other information. We were exhausted and deeply disappointed, feeling responsible to our participants for not having provided them the credential we had promised, and completely powerless to have any influence within the university.

I was in shock. How could this have happened? My colleague and I had taught this material together for twenty-five years all over the world, including a decade in a prestigious MBA program. I wrote, "How could it have gone so wrong? What did I do or not do to create this outcome? I have to question everything about the process and my role in it." Despite lots of reassurance from others involved, I was left feeling worse than ever and lost in a way I had never experienced before, no longer sure of either my identity or my competence. I realized they were completely interconnected, my identity resting largely on my professional capabilities and the intellect I had so long and so carefully developed. Here I was again, with the scattered pieces of my career legacy insufficient to the task. I felt like a partial person, missing an essential ingredient for a successful life. I was bereft and bewildered.

And then that same summer I bought a condo in Vancouver that also needed renovating. My landlord had

63

raised the rent to an unaffordable level and the building was to be covered in a tarp for repairs for most of the next year. I found a condo in the next building that had hardly been touched since it was built twenty-five years before, but it had a beautiful view and allowed me to stay in the neighbourhood I had come to love. I was back for the third time in three years in the business of trying to create a home.

From the beginning, it didn't go well. All through the summer I once more struggled with contractors, tradespeople and retailers, as I fashioned yet another lovely space in which I felt an outsider. My repeated attempts to build an external place where I could feel at home continued to fail and frustrate, leading me irrevocably into overpowering loss and confusion. I filled notebooks with my journaling, turning inward to explore my feelings. I meditated, sometimes for a couple of hours a day. I felt unhinged from all that was familiar.

The Preta in Sanskrit is a "hungry ghost," a being with a huge distended belly and a very narrow throat who is afflicted by an insatiable hunger, doomed to never-ending frustration in not being able to satisfy the obsession. I was a hungry ghost in search of home, repeating the same behaviour and expecting a different outcome. What was happening to me?

They say there are always threshold guardians, the people and processes that hold us fast to our current way of being, preventing us from stepping across the threshold into new worlds. We are attached to the way things are, even when they're not so great. "Better the devil you know," as the saying goes. In my case, there were several guardians holding me at the gate of profound change.

First, I had a very comfortable life surrounded by friends and family, a life of privilege and abundance, travel and excitement. How could I be anything but grateful and happy? Also, I had the strong feeling that if I just persisted, I could make a home and a harmonious place to be. I had the education and experience to create beautiful places. I had done it many times. And finally, I didn't want to further upset my fragile relationship with my husband. We had been together for twenty years—had been happy, busy, carefree, and adventurous. I was convinced we could work it out. We were just at different stages, him still happily working all the time and me retiring from work and not yet sure of what my future held in store.

And yet . . . and yet I knew at some level that I would have to leave this materially comfortable life, to stand on my own and face the unknown, confront my fears and learn whatever lesson I was being drawn to. With a slowly dawning awareness I began to acknowledge that my knowing, my arrogance, my persistence, was at the root of the problem, a recurring theme in my life over the past few years. I wondered how I could not have seen it before. I had to question all my assumptions about myself. Everything I knew to be true probably wasn't. I realized I was in a darkness I had never known. I felt truly afraid.

The Underworld

Loss and Mourning: Deaths and Endings

My ego's humiliation came in many forms over this period, one challenge after another mounting constantly on top of one another, strangely in sets of three. There were the three renovations to my physical homes, each a dismal failure. There were the three disconnects—from my sense of home, from my previous work in the world, and from my relationship. I have come to understand that the number three abounds in mythology, the trinity symbolizing integration, the transcending of the opposing poles in our psyche. In mythological stories, the number three appears frequently, as in the three stages of Descent, Underworld and Ascent in the transformational journey or the Three Fates in Greek and Roman mythology. Psychoanalyst and author Marion Woodman says the feminine always comes in threes. Her concept of "conscious femininity" sees the soul as the reconciling third between the body and spirit, the material and divine.[3] Of course, I had no sense of this in the moment. It is only now that I see the number of triads throughout my journey, perhaps reflecting my disconnection and symbolizing my yearning for feminine inclusion and wholeness.

Another startling example of threes was the deaths, two sets of three, piled up like cordwood. Within eighteen months, six people close to me died. Two deaths were in older age—my dear friend's father and my mother-in-law, who had been a surrogate mother to me for many years. These deaths came close behind my younger cousin who died of cancer within a few months of my arrival in Vancouver. I had spent many summers with her when we were children and I mourned the loss of her friendship. Then, a few months later, the three-month-old baby of a niece suddenly developed a brain swelling and died. While I was reeling from this loss, two colleagues about my own age also died. Both had been mentors at work and school, one a boss and then business partner, and the other a teaching and consulting partner with whom I had written a book.

Suddenly, death was everywhere. I could no longer deny or turn away from it as I had done since my mother died. My grief was overwhelming. I seemed to move from bedside to bedside saying goodbye to loved ones, not able to mourn each one before another was at hand. I began to read voraciously to understand why I felt like I was dying too, each death taking a piece of me into the unknown. I didn't know what to make of it—the piling up of bodies of loved ones, over and over again being confronted with death and dying.

Like most people, I had contemplated death but never at more than a superficial level. I had never really examined my beliefs or considered my choices. I had experienced mystical moments in nature and periodic contact with the ineffable. But I had given up religion as a young adult and not seriously considered my spirituality since. And now, the stark reality of death in the corner of every moment about to pounce on another of my dear ones—or even worse, on me—was a real and constant terror. What did I believe about death and what happened after life?

I felt worn out and worn down. It was just one thing after another in an unending series of bad luck, bad decisions, and bad timing, tumbling over each other as my life crumbled in front of me. I was lost. I found myself in Vancouver, a beautiful city but one I didn't know, often on my own, geographically and emotionally cut off from former friends, colleagues and connections back in Toronto. My son and his family were very generous, but they had their own lives to live. I had left my work behind and when I had tried to recreate it with the university coach training program, it fell apart too. I had lost my power to have sway in the world. I felt alternately depressed and flat, like I was dead too, then easily frustrated and angered, out of control.

There were physical challenges too, telling me I had also lost control of my body. In addition to the long recovery of my knee from the ski accident, I broke both my baby toes during this period. My body was sending messages about brokenness that matched my emotional state. I also had several periods where, as a Type I diabetic, I was unable to control my low blood sugar episodes. I was quite often disoriented, anxious and confused, sometimes sinking into hallucinations, and from time to time I lost consciousness completely, resulting in hospital visits.

On a group trip to Nicaragua to build a school, I lapsed into a coma during sleep on the final night, my blood sugar so low that it took a couple of hours and repeated attempts to fill me with sugar before I came around. I remember slowly regaining consciousness and wondering why I was shivering so hard, being covered in blankets and hugged by our host to warm me, while my husband and our host's wife bustled about our hotel room preparing sugared drinks. I couldn't speak clearly or swallow more than sips. I was aware that I had come close to my own limits. At one point during this period, I could no longer trust myself to be alone with my young grandsons, a loss of sweet intimacy I found hard to bear.

Further, I had terrible nightmares for a year, horrifying dreams that seemed to come from some unbelievably dark, destructive place in me, waking me shaking in horror.

I want to get back to the garden. I step through the window and it shuts behind me. A man and I are cleaning up last year's dead leftovers and planting some new things, cutting the edge to get the path right. We are in a little lowered patch, with the slope moving up behind us. I step back onto a flat place where I can get some perspective. I see what looks like an old log in the dead leaves. I nudge it and it doesn't move. Then I look a

*little closer and realize it's a huge snake
stretching way around the curve of the
garden to the left, hidden by the bushes.
Just then the man steps over toward the
snake and picks up its dead tail and tosses it
into the garden beyond me. I step up the
slope and draw back in horror. He laughs.
"It's dead," he says as he picks up the huge
body and hurls it up the slope at me. I shriek
as the snake lands at my feet and then begins
to coil around my leg with its rotten end. I
wake up shuddering uncontrollably.*

Many of the dreams had masculine and feminine
symbolism, like the snake and the garden, and life and death
references, like cleaning out the old for the new. Many had
erotic aspects and overtones, including snakes, which Freud
saw as phallic symbols.

Sometimes, the dreams not directly horror-filled
included feces, reminding me that I was in "deep shit."

*I am being tortured by someone, a man, who
is just interested in my suffering. I am in a
construction site where work is going on, but
no one pays attention to me. He watches me
struggling to reach the top of a large hole he
has thrown me in that is almost impossible to*

emerge from. I get to the point where I can
almost pull myself over the top when he
appears and puts rocks and feces around the
edge so I have to crawl over them. It is
humiliating and defeating. I know if I win this
one, I'll just be back in the same space again,
having to face another challenge. I know I
am strong, but I feel overwhelmed by it all.

I awoke from this dream in the fetal position with my pillow wet from tears.

In addition to the loss of loved ones, the deterioration of my health, and the terrorizing dreams, there was my failing relationship. My husband and I tried counselling. I spent time on my own. We tried to talk and couldn't connect. Our worlds were growing further and further apart, me on this mysterious inner path neither of us understood and him hoping for a return to some recognizable form of the status quo. I sensed that it was just a matter of time before we had to separate but I didn't have the energy or the courage to make the break. I was still clinging to the notion of home, although that, too, seemed to be slipping away. I was in the unknown without a map or bearing, completely ungrounded.

That spring, I arrived back in Vancouver to my newly renovated apartment expecting to sink into this peaceful haven I hadn't even lived in yet. Two days after I arrived, I heard a dripping sound and realized it was water soaking through the ceiling, running through the new chandelier and bouncing off the dining table onto the newly laid wood floor. This was the beginning of five months of horror as all the work I had done the previous summer was torn apart because of a negligent renovation in the condo above me. Sections of the ceiling collapsed in the living room, dining room and kitchen. Three major air blowers were brought in and plastic enclosures were created around the worst spots to dry it out. The noise was incredible and there was nowhere that wasn't under siege. I also noticed dripping in the master bathroom. Again, the wall had to be removed and another huge blower installed. This time, in taking off the baseboard, a misplaced brad was pulled out of the main water pipe in the wall with the result that the hole flooded the two apartments below me, causing water damage in the thousands of dollars for which I was responsible. Things just kept compounding . . .

These losses further eroded my sense of connection with the world and with myself. I had disintegrated, a piece at a time, in every aspect of my life. Whoever I had been— and I wasn't at all sure I even knew her—was gone. That person had died.

I mourned the loss of her certainty, her power and control, her capacity to take charge with confidence. I had none of that now. How could it all have evaporated so quickly? Or had it been an illusion all along? I realized that all the development work I had done exploring my shadow, which was supposed to have allowed me to know myself, was just the tip of the iceberg. This was a dark destruction I had never known and couldn't even have imagined. And I knew that it was, at some level, my own dark feminine energy—disrupting, destroying, carelessly and selfishly demanding . . . what? Acknowledgement? Reconciliation?

For the next year, I played dead. I was overwhelmed by loss and confusion. I turned inward, became very still, spent much of my time in solitude, read and wrote, dreamed and meditated, was silent. From the outside looking in, you might not have noticed I wasn't myself. I looked the same, I dressed and spoke and kept up with events. But it was a false front, like the old Western movie sets, with nothing behind the façade. I did some therapy, attended several retreats, and surfaced to check in with the world but was really only a wraith, waiting, waiting for daybreak. It was like an unending eclipse where darkness had blocked out the sun and taken with it all hope of a returning light, leaving me shrouded in doubt, feelings of hopelessness, fear, and lack of meaning.

The Discarded Other: My Mother

It was during this apparently lowest of times, what the alchemists call the black blacker than black, the incomprehensible darkness, that I had a glimpse of wonder that changed my life. The friend with whom I had been leading the workshops on developing consciousness invited me to a week-long shamanic retreat in the south-western United States, a deep dive into my consciousness. It was an incredibly revelatory experience, far beyond anything I could have imagined, connecting me to an exquisite unified cosmic reality that I was part of. It thrilled me with its endless interconnections, its beautiful graceful harmony, its combined fragility and strength. Each of the divination journeys over the course of the week gave me an invocation I could explore, the insights exactly what I needed at exactly this moment to begin to wash off all the hurts, disappointments, and old scripts so I could live in "compassionate embrace" of myself, others and the world.

I had several windows into my childhood that shed new light on my discarded feminine. One was when I was about four. I was at my granny's cottage in Chelsea for dinner and I had wandered off while the adults talked. I found a mirror and began to twirl around, my arms holding out my skirt as I spun, boldly saying aloud, "Aren't I beautiful!" I heard laughter and turned to see my aunts giggling at the door. Of course, they were lovingly amused by my performance, but I felt ridiculed for my expressive display of femininity. It breaks my heart even now to feel the shame I felt as that little girl. Another memory of my childhood that came to me was my older brother daring me to do things that were not allowed, like climbing on the roof or stealing cookies. When I resisted, he would say, "Don't be a pussy!" As a child, I thought of this as being a "scaredy cat" and he probably did too. It was only in the reliving of these moments that I realized it also meant don't be a girl, don't be feminine. These examples helped me understand that discarding my feminine had begun very early in life and had created wounds that needed healing.

The most profound moments of the week came with the reconnection to my mother. I saw that she had loved me and had tried her best, in the ways she knew how, to bond with me. I realized that I had been angry at her, feeling her abandonment of me when I was a child as my older brother captured most of the attention. I knew she had done her best to meet all of our needs but saw how I had become tough and independent at a very young age. In fact, I had abandoned her as much as she had abandoned me. Through my teens I had been indignant, defiant, petulant. I had shunned every attempt she made to reach me. I saw her working late into the evening to sew a flowing white chiffon dress with a companion brocade cape for my prom, and the pink suit with the Jackie Kennedy pillbox hat she tailored for my first job interview. I remembered the overflowing table of homemade food lovingly prepared for my birthday party with a large group of friends, and the beautiful portrait she painted of me at about twelve, looking out the dining room window. So many of these gifts!

Sitting in this powerful stew of realizations, I suddenly felt surrounded by incredibly powerful feminine energy, washing over me with such intense compassion for my suffering that I was at first shocked and reeled back to escape the feelings. However, I knew this was exactly where I needed to go—into the discarded feminine part of me. This was the lesson and the treasure. This was home. Feeling overwhelmed by the love and grace and nurturing all around me, I was eventually able to embody some of the miraculous energy, my own rejected feminine energy, a wondrous intimation of wholeness.

There were many other gifts during the week. I was able to experience my own death as peaceful. I was able to forgive perceived wrongs and feel nothing but gratitude. I had no *hard* feelings; my feelings were soft. I was able to see my work in the world as service. I experienced a huge drop in fear. I understood at a cellular level that there is more—

more than I could ever imagine—and that I can choose my way forward based on this expansiveness.

The week was a turning point in my dark night adventure, a calm knowing that gave me a sense of groundedness in all the chaos, a feeling that all was well at the deepest of levels even though on the surface things were in disarray. I was also beginning to feel that I understood some of what was happening to me, this reconnection with the lost feminine part of myself that was my deepest wound, the one I had to confront, the one that had been calling to me all along, to understand and to heal. I could begin to see the road ahead.

A common theme in my dreams over the next several months had to do with reclaiming the feminine. For example, "I am bending down while cooking at the stove, feeling a little odd and wondering why it is necessary. It makes it difficult to see to stir. Suddenly bullets erupt and are whizzing over my head. I am terrified but I am out of the line of fire."

Afterward I wrote, "Am I cooking something up? Am I cooking with grease? Cooking is a feminine activity. Am I protecting the feminine, the weak sister, from attack by the masculine fire? I'm certainly off center, vulnerable to attack, needing to protect my weak feminine from annihilation."

In another dream, "I am in a battle to save the life of my sister. I am with an army of knights jousting for her life. I am barely able to save her. Then, I am in the house with our two other sisters, both of whom also want her dead. I am trying to protect her and I don't know why they want to kill her."

I wondered if my sister again represented the fragile feminine part of me. Sisters appear frequently in feminine mythology as the two sides of light and dark. In dreams, they are said to reflect a new emotional openness to life. In my case there was clearly a conflict about whether to kill these new emotions or not.

My further reunification with the feminine continued during the second year's shamanic retreat, where I focused more intentionally on awakening the sleeping feminine in me. The image I was shown was a garden, handed down to me through generations of women who had tended it. I felt incredible gratitude for my ancestors, particularly the women in my lineage and especially my mother, for the sacrifices they had made to allow me and my garden to flourish. And I, too, had grown a garden in my family, friends, clients, students, and colleagues, all nourished in some small way by my efforts. I saw myself as this metaphorical garden I had inherited through the ages, with its untended patches where I had been careless with myself and others.

I saw that we are the inheritors of the garden of the world and have been careless with it as well. I understood this garden to be the home I had been searching for, within and without. I understood my role in caring for it. I saw the cycles of births and deaths, both necessary to sustain growth. I realized that early in life I had adapted by splitting off those feminine parts of me that I saw as weak and leaving the garden to be a warrior who was always on high alert to avoid being hurt. Now I needed to return to my garden—to tend it, to help it flourish, to sustain it and me, and to pass it on to others. I felt grateful, liberated, and unified, my heart wide open, inspired to tend the garden in myself, in my relationships, and in the world.

It was now about four years into my dark night. The second week-long retreat was an extension and reinforcement of the previous year: deeper, more exquisite, more revealing. There were many transcendent moments, some of the most incredible of my life. At one point I experienced what I have come to understand as a "mystical marriage." It was an indescribably blissful moment of unity, of intimacy between me as feminine energy and a Christ-like masculine energy. It was not a sexual union but an astonishing explosion of love that in some sense created the world, the All. I was completely shaken by the experience. I didn't know how to understand it. I was even reluctant to share it, it felt so colossal. I knew I had been given an incredible gift.

Having now done some research and found that it is not an uncommon occurrence, I can add Caroline Myss' perspective: "It is all about love melting into love. Its expression is absolutely pure, exceedingly delicate, and gentle. There is no way to describe it."[4] Czech psychiatrist Stan Grof adds, "It usually means that the masculine and feminine aspects of the personality are reaching a new psychological balance."[5]

It was a kind of culmination, a new wholeness that again, changed me as a person. It gave me a direction, a new perspective that fueled my confidence to step out beyond the heavy veil that had been covering me for so long. I knew beyond any doubt that the fabric of the universe was love beyond our imagining. I could see that the route to compassionate embrace came from the heart of the feminine, and I Am That. In contrast to this spark of divinity, or to bring my lofty illumination into more practical down-to-earth terms, I was also encouraged to bring delight to those who were suffering—through play, art, coaching, conversation, all talents I could draw on. I thought perhaps I'd call it something like *The Art of Dying.*

One of the grounding actions I took after the retreat was to convene a couple of what I called Death and Dining dinners. In my grief over the loss of my loved ones, I wanted to talk to others about what I was experiencing but had mostly been urged to get over it. I was beginning to feel like something of an expert on dying, with all my personal experience and reading. This seemed a way to provoke the conversations about this fearful subject with friends I trusted. The dinners turned out well and the discussions were rich and revealing. I felt I was onto something needed in our society. It also felt very good to be doing something outside of myself; I had been turned inward for such a long time.

Before leaving this Underworld stage, I feel it is important to note the many guides and mentors who helped me along the way and who made the journeying bearable and often joyful. Family, friends, colleagues, neighbours, and so many others visited, befriended, witnessed, supported and loved me along the way. They provided the oh-so-necessary others to sustain me and draw me out of my aloneness. Without them, the journey would not have been tolerable. They gave me exactly the kind of help I needed most to start the upward turn.

The Ascent

Rebirth and its Sacrifices: Loss of Innocence

The mythologies say that rebirth requires a sacrifice, a price to be paid for the privilege of returning to the world. For me, one of the sacrifices was my marriage. The last months with my husband were difficult. We led more and more parallel lives, him travelling all the time, me on an inner journey that didn't include him. We knew it was over but neither of us could end it. For me, it was the fear of being on my own, without protection or safety. Who would watch over me? Who would be with me to ensure I didn't harm the grandkids because of my diabetic lows? I found that despite all my illuminations and the promises they held out to me, I was resistant at this stage, too, hesitant to leave my familiar life to begin a new one.

Finally, when the family left after visiting for their annual spring break, I got up the nerve to have the conversation we had avoided for so long. It wasn't an emotional scene. It was a recognition and declaration of what we both knew to be true. I flew home two days after the family, leaving everything behind, and broke the news. No one was shocked, given our recent history. I went with deep mourning, feeling I had done everything I could and failed to make it work. I felt all the stability of my comfortable life ending. I was hurt, disappointed, sad, and afraid. It was like the rug being pulled out from under me as I landed in a heap back in Vancouver to begin again.

There were other sacrifices too. With the end of the relationship, I had to sacrifice all my romantic ideals of how enough love and enough persistence can solve anything. I gave up the last of my innocence about my ability to control events, to solve all problems, to find the easiest way out. I gave up knowing and certainty, the pillars on which my former life was based. And I gave up any sense of being powerful, of bigness in the world. In the end, I sacrificed my former self, the self I had been—the comfortable, confident self who was now a distant memory.

Incredibly, though, the first six months on my own were transformational. I felt buoyant, confident, happy, complete, energetic, and fulfilled. I settled into looking after myself with enthusiasm. I found that I was balanced and calm. I did feel as if I had died to my old life and been born anew. I felt I was in the lunar phase of my life, in the darkness that actually holds the light from which life springs. I wrote, "Just as there is night and day, sun and moon, I am in a dark phase where there is only moonlight, so be in the dark as the moon is in the night and softly light the way back into day."

None of my fears materialized. Quite the contrary, I became more and more fearless, felt more and more grace-filled. My journal noted, "I am a grace-full gardener." I felt immensely grateful for my life and saw each day as a gift. The warm sun, the birdsong, the gentle whisper of the trees. I realized nothing in this world belonged to me—it is all gifts bestowed for me to use for better or worse. I was still, resting after the perilous journey before stepping back into the world.

As my energy increased, so too did my interest in things around me. With my renewed clarity and vitality came a powerful pull to re-enter my larger world, to be of some service, to express my gratitude. Although it was somewhat difficult to leave the blissful home I had inhabited, both within and without, the road back has been full of surprises and delights. I have grown closer to my family and friends, have enjoyed participating in my neighbourhood activities, have travelled, painted, and become fit. I have a new connection to my body, enjoying my movements and good health. I have developed a six-week program called *Dying to Live* to foster conversation about preparing for our death so we can live fully now. I am in a new relationship that brings me great joy. My journals full of words, mostly judgements of myself and others, have been replaced with colourful pictures and poetic invocations. And I understand that the darkness is always with me; my despair and my joy are two sides of the same coin. The moon, the eternal feminine, needs to be fed in both its light and dark phases.

Restoration and Integration: Unity of Body/Mind/Heart

The last year has been a time of restoring a sense of wholeness in my life. The entire dark night process has restored me to my larger Self, integrating the lost feminine and bringing new meaning and congruence to my identity. All of the sacrifices, the necessary losses I have experienced, are gems of growth in my depth of being. It is not over, of course. The process continues to unfold but it is now within a unity of opposites—the dark and the light, the masculine and the feminine, the unconscious and conscious, the spiritual and material—both poles of the psyche always present in a dynamic equilibrium.

I have been restored to my feminine body through dance, a wonderful reconnection with the joy of movement. I danced as a teenager at sock hops during school lunch breaks and at high school dances most weeks. At thirteen, I even won an early transistor radio in a jive contest. And although I have danced on occasion since then and enjoyed it, the opportunities have been few and far between. Now, the thrill of expressing my enjoyment through the freedom of movement is intoxicating—leaping and twirling and sweeping my arms to delicious music, not concerned with how I look but with how I feel. I am that little girl of four in front of the mirror, now set free.

One of my most memorable moments of reuniting with my mother came at a retreat with my dance group in Mexico. It was called *Dancing on our Graves* and with my interest in death, it seemed tailor-made for me. We had been asked to bring a childhood photo for one of the sessions. In the final moments of packing I had thrown a small framed picture of me at about five into my suitcase. It had hung just above my night table for years, moving with me from house to house. When the session came, we were asked to glue the picture onto a collage. Since mine was framed, I turned it over to see how I might take the picture out. There on the back was a faded poem from a newspaper, carefully glued to the frame's paper backing. It is called "A Farewell," written by Charles Kingsley, and obviously cut out and pasted there by my mother before she died.

> *My fairest child, I have no song to give you;*
> *No lark could pipe to skies so dull and grey:*
> *Yet, ere we part, one lesson I can leave you*
> *For every day.*

Be good, sweet maid, and let who will be clever;
Do noble things, not dream them, all day long:
And so make life, death and that vast forever
One grand, sweet song.

I was astounded to find it! How had I not seen it before? Or had I looked at it but not appreciated it as the gift it was? Did it mean my mother knew she was dying? Was she depressed? Was it because of me? How could I not have understood how much she loved me and wanted me to be happy? Had I done the noble things she wished for me?

The poem was cathartic. It allowed me to connect with the loving being she was, the sadness in her life and early death, the care with which she had shared her affection. I loved the last two lines, the idea that life and death were two sides of the same coin, and all part of the "grand, sweet song" of forever. I have used the metaphor of life as one sweet song ever since. It has a special ability to draw me into the place of unity and transcendence, of life death and that vast forever, in every moment.

I have also been restored to my feminine sense of place through my home and neighbourhood. I start most days with a coffee and breakfast in my chair beside the fire. I always have a stack of books, some partly read, some waiting their turn. I read there, I nap, I think, I am quiet there. I do two crosswords on the sofa with my partner. My desk looks out onto the seawall, where life teems with walkers, runners, bikers, strollers, and in good weather, with picnickers on the lawn. I am grateful every day for the privilege of living where I do.

I have learned that my neighbourhood is also an exceptional gift. Not only is it accessible without a car to everything I need, but it is also a unique historical setting in the city, a 1970s leasehold residential redesign of a declining industrial area with mixed-use, medium-density housing and extensive open and public spaces along the creek. It has a lively sense of community, with social events and public participation. I was invited to join the neighbourhood association, an active group of volunteers, and have found it a great way to make new friends and contribute to community projects. We have, for example, brought two refugee families into the neighbourhood and provided housing and financial support over the past couple of years.

I have been restored to a new, more feminine confidence and competence by sharing my experience and understanding of death. The *Dying to Live* workshops have been extremely rewarding and seem to be very helpful to the participants in the conversations. I have written a handbook so the workshop can be delivered by others and shared broadly. I have a new younger co-facilitator and together we offer a six-week program as well as weekend workshops and online courses. The circles have filled through word of mouth. My friends, family and neighbours have not only joined me but have recommended others. We have been able to offer the program over a dozen times so far.

This work feels right for me now, purposeful and contributory. I continue to learn from others' experiences. Sharing stories normalizes death and the dying process, reducing fear, and also encourages completing the necessary preparations so life can be fully lived now. This legacy is a direct result of my dark night journey, a manifestation of the events and insights I am now taking out into the world, sharing the treasure I have been given.

There are more restorations I could name but I will end with the restoration of my sense of my whole Self. It feels like a return to something familiar that I have not experienced before, age-old and yet new. It is sinking into the ordinariness of every day, every small thing, behind which is a great mystery and interconnection. I feel I am softening into what is, as my way of being in the world, acknowledging the integrated darkness and light as always present at every level from my own being out into the vast cosmos. Softening into the unity of the ever-present paradoxes of light and dark, feminine and masculine, inner and outer, individual and collective, welcoming and honouring both as one.

In our culture the dark is feared, repressed, and denied, as is death. Much of our inner life is discounted, especially our inner feminine. This stance rejects the critical role that falling apart and descending into darkness plays in growing and transcending into wholeness. We are crippled by our need for control and certainty. By recognizing that the ups and downs, the falling and rising, the wins and losses, are what life is, we also recognize that there are no happy endings, or tragic ones either. They are all both and one. This leads me into a calm acceptance of how things are and how I am, as a whole and as part of the larger whole.

But it is not a do-nothing stance. Quite the opposite. It frees me to see opportunities all around me to offer my gifts without any expectation. I simply want to give without any need for acknowledgement or return. The gift of giving is that I receive, often in unlikely and unpredictable ways. This to me is my role and contribution now, a calm, open giving from the heart in whatever ways show up—not for power, glory or status, but for the privilege of sharing some of my wisdom from the adventure. In telling my story, I come back to living from this very different perspective, leading from who I am now.

[3] Woodman, Marion. *Conscious Femininity* (Toronto: Inner City Books, 1993), XX

[4] Myss, *Entering the Castle,* 35.

[5] Grof, Christine and Stanislav. *The Stormy Search for the Self* (New York: Penguin, 1990), 87.

Chapter Four
Other Dark Night Stories

Pour yourself out like a fountain.
Flow into the knowledge that what you are seeking
finishes often at the start, and, with ending, begins.
. . . Rainer Maria Rilke

There are many ways to make the dark night passage. As I have begun to talk to friends and acquaintances about my experience, I have enjoyed connecting with them about their distinctive ways of moving through the process. Six of them have bravely agreed to have their stories included here. Their openness and vulnerability make these shorter examples of dark nights revealing windows into both the uniqueness of the journeys and their recurring themes and patterns.

I have loosely arrayed the stories where I believe they best fit each storyteller's stage in the journey, as shown in the figure below.

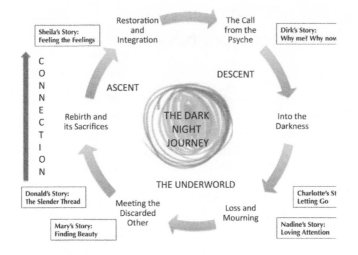

Each story encompasses all the previous stages as we move along. For example, Dirk's story in the Descent is the most partial, as he is at the beginning of the passage. At the other extreme, Sheila's story of her Ascent is the most complete, because she has moved through all of the stages. As mentioned earlier, these dark night categorizations are inexact but will give an approximate flow to the process.

All six are stories of alienation from our current ways of being and the deep work involved in the transformation of our consciousness so that we can reclaim our Discarded Other—whatever key part of ourselves we have ignored or suppressed—and bring ourselves into new wholeness. In the Descent stories, Dirk and Charlotte, this Discarded Other is only a dim outline in the loss and confusion. In the

Underworld stories, Nadine and Mary, the Discarded Other takes shape and is confronted, heralding a new birth. In the Ascent stories, Donald and Sheila, the Discarded Other has been welcomed into our consciousness and we reconnect with the world from a new spaciousness of perspective.

I have used direct quotes from my conversations with the storytellers as much as possible, adding my perspective to tease out the potential underlying meanings. What stands out for me, perhaps because it mirrors my own story, is that each vignette has something to do with reclaiming the lost feminine, whether the storyteller is male or female, whether its shape is love, self-worth, creativity, relationships, feelings, or simply moving from alienation to connection, to finding home. Just as I have reinterpreted the stories, I invite you to do the same as you engage with them.

Stories of Descent

Dirk's Story: Why Me? Why Now?

In a real dark night of the soul it is always three o'clock in the morning, day after day.
. . . F. Scott Fitzgerald

Sometimes, the call comes not gradually as a dawning presence but instantly as a shocking rupture that suddenly changes everything in our world. A health crisis, an accident, an unexpected death—all can initiate the plunge into a dark night beyond our control. It is an emergency call and we must respond, often from a place of incomprehension and disbelief.

Imagine. You are out for your morning walk, moving along at your usual crisp pace, when suddenly you feel like you're going to fall. It's not dizziness, more a strange feeling of not being able to stay upright. You slough it off and keep going, even though you know this isn't a good sign. Then you feel better until, again, the weird feeling comes back. You're going to fall. You'd better head home.

This was the beginning of Dirk's stroke. He says, "I had to concentrate hard on the footpath in front of me to get a visual triangulation to stop me falling, to focus on my balance."

Dirk knew the signs of stroke but by the time he got home, he felt fine and had breakfast. It was when his speech started to slur that he and his wife decided they had better go to the local health center. It didn't take more than a few questions for the staff to confirm that Dirk was having a stroke. He was taken to the local hospital. He says of this time, "We chatted and had a laugh in the ambulance, I was testing my lungs, moving my arms around, and it was fine, but they kept telling me I was having a stroke."

After a series of specialist consultations, including conferring with a stroke center, there was no clear decision about what Dirk needed. He could have the heavy drugs to burst any clots in his brain, but there were potentially severe side effects. Or he could take a series of medications and let things run their course. He opted for the medications but didn't feel he needed all of them. Even as he was wheeled off to a ward, he could move his limbs and speak, things he felt he wouldn't be doing if he were having a stroke. He was in denial.

After a fitful sleep, he woke up to find his whole left side paralyzed and his speech very slurred. Just as he was becoming aware of these restrictions, a doctor walked in and asked him how he was doing. He reacted in anger. "Well, how do you think I'm doing? My left hand doesn't work, I can't speak, I can't stand, but apart from that, I'm absolutely wonderful!" With that emotional outburst, Dirk began to realize how the stroke had, overnight, changed his life. "Hold on, that means I won't be able to go walking any more, I certainly won't be able to play tennis or table tennis, and all of the bright lights of my life disappeared, just like that." He was in the darkness. Dirk reflects, "The dark night crept up on me while I slept."

Dirk is seventy, a New Zealander, a retired sound engineer, business owner and corporate logician. He is analytical but wears his heart on his sleeve. He says he suffers from a lack of self-appreciation. I found him engaging and outspoken. He has been through the usual ups and downs in life but sees the stroke as by far the darkest night he has known. It was a shock to him and everyone around him. "No one could understand why I had had a stroke. I ate well and was fit, not an apparent candidate for one at all."

Dirk was in hospital for a month, where he underwent intense physiotherapy to regain enough movement in his hands, arms and legs so that he could have some assisted mobility. There was improvement almost from the beginning. "At first, I couldn't move a finger. Then just a little, little bit. Then a little bit more. These tiny changes became mountains to climb and I challenged myself to do the work." He says of this period, "It was horrible. I hated it. It was mind-numbingly boring and repetitive." He felt the darkness all around him: the depression, the frustration, the grief. "Sometimes when I was doing the exercises, it just wouldn't happen; one finger wouldn't work. All the other fingers were moving. It was hugely depressing to see it, that finger just wouldn't move, as if no one was telling it what to do."

But his dedication paid off. Dirk managed to walk unaided from the hospital to the car. He has recently begun riding his electric bike again despite a setback when his daughter visited. They went for a short ride, although Dirk knew he was pushing his luck. He had a difficult time getting on and off the bike. At the end of the ride, as he got off, he fell and hit his head hard. He now has a concussion that has further eroded his capacities, making him very tired yet unable to sleep well, and adding to the darkness. "The darkness is holding me where I am and I'm not sure of that reasoning yet."

One of Dirk's saving graces is that he has been a meditator for forty years and has a strong belief system as a result of his practice. He has been to India many times to be part of a community of kindred spirits. Despite how bad it seems as he considers all he has lost, he says of his spirituality, "I do have that in the background as somewhere to go." He comments that the stroke has answered the question he has long asked himself about why he meditates. He knew only that he had to, but now he can see that the practice has allowed his consciousness to come to terms with the dark night, to see the spark of hope even when he has felt quite bitter, all his pleasures seeming to have been ripped from him in an instant.

> Meditation gives you quite a heightened self-
> awareness so facing something like this, it
> gives you two views. One is looking at the
> larger view, the karmic account of this event.

The other is living in the body and trying to work on the physical day-to-day level. The two viewpoints allow me to visit the darkness on these different planes. How can I raise my level of thinking above the day-to-day and see the positive to come, despite the massive losses of ability?

This journey is so unique to the person, but it is important to know that stepping outside of yourself and looking back in allows you to work through most of the darkness without actually putting the bag over your head.

Dirk says that he is well into the Darkness stage of his dark night journey. He comments, "Unfortunately the self-awareness I have been growing is nowhere to be found in the deepest of these dark places, and the horizon with its expected high remains sternly invisible." He admits he expected that because he has done long-term meditation, the dark night wouldn't be such a problem, but it is. "Meditation doesn't stop you getting into the dark parts; they occur regardless of what I think or do." However, despite his disappointment, he adds, "If I'd looked into myself before the stroke, I would have thought it could be a lot worse than it really is, so something to do with the long-term meditation means I am able to be aware of what is happening and live through it."

Dirk has a new curiosity about astrology. "The knowing of 'why me' and 'why now' is in some part answered by my newfound interest in astrology, this being quite sudden and intense, with the sense there are forces at work that we, at best, only aspire to understand." He has done a deep dive into this new territory.

> *I don't have a complete handle on it, but I know it is part of something that is not just Dirk or Dirk and his friends and family. The events are cyclic and visible on a bigger level than just the individual and that helps me take a bigger view of where I am, as opposed to getting so totally lost in the deep dark stuff.*

Where Dirk will go from here in his dark night journey is unclear. Through his astrological enquiry and his meditation, he may be able to discern the hidden Discarded Other who waits in the deep dark, yearning for recognition. As he says, what is holding him in the dark is as yet unknown. Perhaps it is that self-appreciation he says he is currently lacking. "Lack of self-esteem plays a huge part in the dark night for me."

What is clear is that Dirk is no longer the person he has been. He has many questions, including "Why me?" and

"Why now?" but also "Who am I?" and "Where am I headed?" Grappling with these questions requires a rethinking of his meaning-making system, of his identity. This is the work he is engaged in and it will take time. Through the stroke he has been forced into a confrontation with his deepest self. He needs space to catch up to himself, to allow the mourning that is necessary to honour the losses, to settle into the experience and begin to see it from different perspectives, to place it in his life story, to discern the patterns and make sense of them. His strong belief system and his meditation will assist. At the end of the day, the darkness will give up its light—the light of understanding, of wholeness. Holding that possibility is a scaffold when things have fallen apart.

Charlotte's Story: Letting Go

> *Everyone can master grief but (she) that has it.*
> **... William Shakespeare**

Charlotte's story begins deeper into the dark night. She has been in the Darkness stage for some time, feeling the unraveling of her former life and the loss of control over events. Nothing seems to bring satisfaction. This is a stage that is often confused with depression, and it is important to distinguish between the two. True depression, as Charlotte says in her story, needs professional treatment. The temporary depression that is part of grieving our former life is a natural occurrence in the deep darkness.

Charlotte wrote to me the day before our meeting to say she couldn't talk. "I am in such a sad place that I need to postpone our appointment. I think when you are *in* a dark night it isn't going to work. I am filled with such sadness and with tears that never seem to end." After some encouragement, she decided to speak anyway and her telling of her dark night story opened my heart. I was aware as she spoke of her very expressive face, her beautifully polished speaking style, and her ready infectious laugh, even in the midst of her gloom.

She began her career as an actress in London theatre and television, moving on to become a successful international voice and media trainer and consultant. She lived in Singapore for twenty years, working with government and industry leaders across Asia on public speaking, media exposure, and communication skills. Then a recession hit and Charlotte decided to study in the US, resulting in five years of commuting between Singapore, California and the UK to maintain work, study, and family connections. She had hoped to base herself in the US but when her two-year application and subsequent appeal to get a green card was turned down after 9/11, she felt called to return home to London, feeling "bereft and defeated," to build a life closer to family. She says, "When I have periodically hit these dark pits in the past, I have eventually been able to climb out through activity. But my previous lifelines—my life and work in Singapore and with the Tibetan community in the foothills of the Himalayas, my friends in North America, my family—all these are under threat for various reasons."

Charlotte entered this darkness not long after returning to London, realizing that it did not give her the feeling of home she had hoped for. She wrestled with finding a sense of peace and place. "I've never made England work for me. I don't really fit here." She tried a book group, an art class, a women's circle, and being a college trustee, but none worked for her. Now in her mid-seventies, she finds it more difficult to travel to be with friends in other parts of the world where she feels more at home, and the costs are high too. "The preparation and recovery time from long-distance travel across time zones and changes in climate take their toll. The Internet helps but we oldies long to be in the same room!"

She was recently asked to be an Elder in her Quaker community but felt she would be able to fulfill the significant duties and responsibilities only at the expense of visiting her family outside London and being able to travel to be with friends. She feared becoming even more alienated, rather than fulfilled by it. Further, she didn't feel she truly fit in. "I have never really felt I belonged or that they knew who I was. The people and the Meetings for Worship themselves don't bring me joy. Sometimes it feels like a complete loss of faith."

In one of our email exchanges following our conversation, Charlotte revealed that her father had been "the embodiment of a Quaker." A thought struck her. She loved what she witnessed of his faith but struggled because of changes since his time. "It is not easy to love and accept the way things have developed. There are aspects of modern Quakerism that would have astonished and infuriated my dad, who would have been writing and speaking his objections!" Was she afraid that walking away from the community would mean losing some part of him? Was she clinging to his certainty? Should she be mounting her own crusade, or was it too late in the day and in her life? She is full of questions, searching for her place in the world as her formerly busy life fades and her activities diminish.

I have a sense during our conversation that Charlotte may be entering the Underworld as she recounts stories, one after another, of loss and mourning. Illness, accidents, family dynamics, lack of connection and lack of energy: all have resulted in losses. Some of these are current, others some time ago. As often happens during the dark night, our previous losses must be endured all over again. She has lost six friends in plane and train crashes and car accidents, her nephew dropped dead at thirty-eight, leaving a six-month-old baby, her Chinese son's seven-year-old daughter died agonizingly of brainstem cancer, a lifelong friend has withered after losing her husband, a soul mate has pancreatic cancer.

Lately, Charlotte has become estranged from her oldest son and his family. She says, "I cannot imagine a time when I could come to terms with having them gone from my life." With each of these losses, she describes "a light going out" in her life, a disconnection from her sense of purpose and joy. She refers to "the terminal nature of life," of friendships, of what calls to us, what engages us, what brings us pleasure. "What I'm feeling now is sadness. It feels like permanent loss, whether that loss is the loss of myself, my way of life, my family, my friends, my working life or my God." She reflects on her aloneness, "I don't have anyone I can call. It's like being stuck in the middle of the Sahara. I can't find the people who make me laugh and feel light. And I don't know where to go looking for that right now."

As we begin to discuss the distinctions between a dark night and depression, Charlotte talks about how the depression she experienced earlier in life felt.

It seems to me that depression is powerless whereas grief, sadness and loss are full of power and meaning. Depression is locked in. It fractures me. It terrifies me. It distorts and separates. It paralyses me, as if life is literally sucked out of me. I am imprisoned by depression. It is out of my control until the time of my release and I don't know if that will ever happen. It is as if everything has ceased to have any meaning. Depression appears empty because all hope has gone.

I ask Charlotte about the deep grief she is feeling now and how it is different from depression.

Unlike depression, which can often be completely dysfunctional—you really are under the duvet with no will—in this darkness you can go through the motions of functioning. You can make a plan, go play tennis, travel and be in the world, but the default is always there when you come back. It is an effort to go and be normal somewhere and hit a tennis ball and make conversation. You come home and there is this loss of energy. The only pleasure I get is going out in the garden to cut deadheads, to be in nature.

Charlotte pauses to collect her thoughts and then continues to describe her feelings.

> *This sadness, loss, and grief well up from inside me, unbearable, raw, powerful and unquenchable. It is sometimes an exquisite pain. Where depression is sans life, sadness and grief are the torrent of extreme, unleashed feeling, a life force. This is active possession, exhausting, punishing, persistent. It can be diverted, suspended even, but only temporarily. It must run its course.*

As I listen to this description, I wonder if she is feeling what Sufi healer Angela Fischer describes as feminine longing. "The aching emptiness, need to be loved, sense of loss or incompletion that women so often experience as second nature can be the longing to go Home, the longing of what is real calling for them to return."[6]

Charlotte suddenly shifts gears and talks about a glimmer of hope, "a thread of a silver lining." She has a new neighbour, an American woman, whom she met in front of their terraced Georgian townhouses returning home with groceries. "That very day we had coffee and it turns out she knows places I know, we have a lot in common. We sat in my kitchen and drank coffee and cried together. I'm hoping she is a new friend."

As we come to the end of the conversation, Charlotte admits, "The grief, the loss, is a very private thing and it's only with somebody I'm close to that I can share it at all. I wouldn't attempt to reveal the depth of the way I'm feeling with anybody who cannot grasp the reality of it. They might understand if you had a partner who died, if there was a justifiable grief."

It is perhaps not surprising that Charlotte, who is half Russian Jew, refers to Chekhov. "He understood. Masha in Uncle Vanya talks about being in mourning for her life. Maybe there's something in the Russian psyche that understands deep grief and the necessity of being in it." I feel privileged that Charlotte has shared her private troubles with me from a place of being in the throes of dying to her former self, her former life, in her private darkness.

Charlotte is not certain how her next steps in the dark night journey will unfold, what Discarded Other she is to meet. She is currently mourning the terminal nature of everything in life that must eventually die in order for us to be reborn into more of who we can potentially be. "I have to find a way to accept that there is no way back and I can never have what I had. I have to transform the love, safety, satisfaction, the joy, the feeling that all's right with the world into something that is integrated and part of my internal existence. It has to become a bonus rather than a loss."

She reflects, "It may be something about a transformation from an active external world into a rich and meaningful internal world, the world of experience, imagination and contemplation. Shedding stuff. Letting go." Time will tell how this rich internal world will unfold. Right now, Charlotte is on her way to a funeral of an elderly friend whose family she has known since the age of thirteen. I am reminded of T.S. Eliot's famous line about deep grief, "A condition of complete simplicity (Costing not less than everything)"[7]

Stories of The Underworld

Nadine's Story: Loving Attention

Life shrinks or expands in proportion to one's courage.. . .
Anaïs Nin

I met Nadine on Granville Island near my home for our conversation. I talked her into a couple of donut holes from Lee's, a treat I give myself when I'm at the market, and we sat eating them at an outdoor table with the trucks and the tourists creating a background cacophony that didn't seem to interrupt our flow. She spoke with such energy and good humour, reflecting back on the provocative experiences through her dark night, I suspected immediately that she had turned a corner in her journey.

Nadine says she operates at the "frontier of possibilities" as a social innovator, a big-picture thinking partner, transformational consultant and leadership coach. Starting out in science and technology, she has become an entrepreneur and teacher in organization and executive development. She hails from New Zealand and like me has been a vagabond most of her life, living and working in many parts of Canada as well as in her native country. Recently, after a sabbatical back in New Zealand, she has settled on Vancouver Island, a place she says feeds her soul. I ask Nadine to give me a sense of her dark night journey.

My sense is that I have had three significant calls from the underworld since I turned forty. The most recent call began when I left Toronto. It really felt more like I was being kicked out. I was being pushed out of my comfort zone, out of my normal way of doing things, and invited to leave home. When I sold my house, packed three suitcases, gave away most of the rest and left, there was a very uncomfortable disorientation. I had nowhere to go. I was letting go of control, planning and everything that had created such a cognitively comfortable way of operating.

I see again in Nadine an over-dependence on masculine qualities that eventually leads to a call for integration.

The events leading up to this departure from Toronto were a series of mishaps, accidents and surprises that began on a retreat. Participants were asked to ritualize letting go and then write something they wanted to release on a piece of paper and throw it into a fire. Nadine wrote, "Life as I know it." As she says, "Be careful what you ask for!" A sequence of events over twelve months ended with the three suitcases and no plan about what was next.

The first notable event was an insight during a meditation to "Get on your bike and ride." Feeling rather skeptical, Nadine rode through the Toronto ravine system to the waterfront, all the while worrying that a client would see her taking the afternoon off. This was a work day! While riding, she heard herself say, "Fire yourself." She thought, "What a novel idea! My entire life has been about addiction to work, so as a first step I'm going to stop pursuing business and see what happens."

A couple of months later the second event unfolded. She was sitting having coffee at home, her dog beside her, when lightning struck the house. "I was sitting in the kitchen just a few feet away from the metal railing around the deck when it hit. All the electronics were destroyed: computers, Internet, phones, garage door openers, printers, appliances.

Nothing worked. I was told it would take six weeks to replace my Internet so I was essentially out of business."

Two months after that, in a third event, someone rear-ended her car and although she was told at the hospital that nothing was physically wrong, she felt all her cells had been rearranged. Six weeks later while she was getting a massage, the masseur commented, "If you weren't so strong, you'd be a total mess." She replied, "I think I am!"

The final straw came with a strong sense that she should sell her house. She had been discouraged by the slowness of her home repairs and her loss of work. However irrational it seemed, she decided to act. She put her house on the market and was staggered when it sold in a week at full price despite being quite a unique design. "I put my bare essentials in storage, had a party with friends, and left. I had resisted the call until there was nothing else to do." Nadine notes that through this period there were so many helpers who came just at the right time. "It was such a surprise, having always been very independent and finding it hard to ask for help. It seemed like a miracle that those last days went so smoothly."

She went back to New Zealand, not knowing where else to go, and began to read, reflect, and try to understand what she was experiencing. "Everything was foggy, unclear. I didn't know where I belonged, who my deepest connections were with, what I could rely on or what I should be doing, if anything. I wasn't even grounded in the practical day-to-day sense; everything was more onerous." Jane Meredith writes about this sense of being totally lost, "The Underworld gets some bad press. We associate it with helplessness, pain, fear, depression and despair. This is at least partly because we so strongly resist and delay visiting these dark and difficult places of confronting the truth of our lives. We have a backlog to deal with when we are finally forced into it."[8]

Nadine had resisted these calls for years and was now being forced to contend with the consequences.

And things kept happening. She bought her mother tickets to the Russian ballet for Mother's Day but when she got there, the ballet was cancelled. She signed up for a meditation retreat and when she arrived, she was the only person there, alone in the room. On a rain-soaked windy day, when her umbrella turned inside out, a stranger picked it off the ground and put it in the garbage. He said he was going home. She responded, "I'm going home too!"

Nadine returned to Canada and settled on Vancouver Island, but things only got darker. She tried half a dozen times without success to buy a home and when she finally closed a deal, the owner couldn't be found to sign papers. She created yet another big project she called

"Enterprising Women," designed to help women dealing with abuse, poverty, and addiction to restart their lives. But she says, "I was still impatient, not trusting the flow, and there was no traction."

When the financial crisis hit, business in North America evaporated and without contacts on the west coast, she decided if she had to start over, she would do it in New Zealand. There, she says, "the whole thing started to happen again: a guy crashed into my car for no reason, consulting seemed to be a local game, and I couldn't find a place to call home." Nadine also had physical challenges—intense pain resulting from an undiagnosed crack in her pelvis, then the need for a hip replacement. "At that stage I was at my lowest. I'd say, 'If I die, I don't really care, I'm done. It's too hard.'"

But after surgery and intensive rehab for a year, she slowly recognized a shift in her energy, the first signs of a rebirth. She felt "unleashed in a different way with a sense of groundedness, resilience, availability for life." The quiet time had allowed her to see the magic in the darkness. "It was a huge insight for me that I don't need to be creating some big idea, just small, simple and personal is OK, just my own intention and attention." Jean Shinoda Bolen names this quality "a spiritual center or inner presence that warms and illuminates your psyche and your body. You will have a feeling of being at home in yourself."[9] It seems to me that Nadine, as she moves away from reliance on the cognitive, doing, masculine aspects of herself, is taking on the more feminine qualities of home-and hearth.

When I asked Nadine about what Discarded Other she has to face to move forward, she says it's about self-worth, giving and receiving love. She comments that she has lived in her head for her first forty years.

I was the little fat kid and only felt acknowledged for being the first in sports or in academics. It was all about achievement and I didn't have a sense anybody cared beyond that. For me, it has been about the layers and layers of unraveling the lovable, connected me and my ability to love in all dimensions—the cosmic, the familial, the collegial—and to bring that into the world.

Nadine says now, seven years later and back in Canada, she has a strong sense of who she is at this stage but is still challenged to know how she wants to be in the world, what her rebirth might look like.

I think it's about lightness, playfulness, freedom, a sense of connection. Work was the center of my life and through this dark night I have had very little work but a lot of learning. I realize I've been spending sixty hours a week with little money or clients to show for it. I've learned to understand patience, trust and being rather than doing, at completely new levels. Currently, I'm embracing the idea of being as an invitation for something to come, energetically or psychologically. It's a big shift for me to trust my intuition, go with what feeds me, that things unfolding in such mysterious ways is perfect, I don't need to always cognitively sort it out.

She acknowledges that she still sometimes doubts but is learning to accept the way things are while holding her course. "I've never been particularly religious but unless I have a very wild imagination there is something else going on that is much bigger than me." This kind of surrender to what is without undue pressure or expectation is characteristic of moving into the rebirth process, of new insight and understanding of a larger whole.

Perhaps Nadine is not through her dark night journey, but as she begins life again in Canada she is finding deep friendships that seem to have been waiting for her. She says, "There is still an occasional wobble and fear the deep dark will return but I am finding confidence again, recognizing this is a place I feel at home, some familiarity and peace, both internally and in relation to the exterior world, in a very different way than I've ever experienced before. I'm not sure I've understood the sacrifice, but I feel like I'm ready to integrate, open, blossom and flourish."

She is also learning to be satisfied with simple little things rather than pushing for big strategic change. "Love, after all, is being content with exactly what is, paying attention to the ordinary things in life, like a conversation with donut holes! It's all part of being, like the day and night, it's a natural cycle and there's as much treasure in the dark as in the light."

Mary's Story: Finding Beauty

We do not become artists. We came as artists. We are.
Some of us are still catching up to what we are.
 . . . **Clarissa Pinkola Estes**

"I am feeling energized, curious, bold, with some moments of fear." Mary begins with these words and I am immediately excited to hear her story. These are the kinds of feelings associated with emerging from the Underworld after meeting the Discarded Other. She is seeing everything with new eyes, beginning to re-member after a time of coming apart. Mary is eager to try her new wings and fly.

Her transformation is what I have come to call a dark night "lite," that is, she is making the transition, becoming more whole, taking on a discarded part of herself, and doing so with relative ease, although not without anxiety and fear of the future. It can be done! She describes how, through her own dark journey, this came to be.

> *I left my job as CEO of a southern American*
> *nonprofit about six months ago. I had been*
> *bored for the previous five years, working too*
> *hard and playing too little. I felt like I was*
> *pushing a large boulder up a mountain,*
> *taking responsibility for far more than I*
> *wanted to. My days had a heaviness to them*
> *that weighed me down. Finally, eighteen*

119

months ago, I answered the call to a more
balanced way of life, enrolling in a coach
training program, looking for a job transition.
I had been a consultant for ten years prior to
my CEO role and thought I would again like
my own business but this time with coaching
as the main offering.

As Mary describes her life today, her face lights up.
She is enthusiastic and optimistic. "I currently have five
clients and I am taking an accelerated business development
program that will help me shape my company. My coaching
is about helping women to go deep, connecting them to
their authentic selves, which is very satisfying work. I find it
is a reflection of my own process of self-development."

When I ask about her fears, she says her previous
anxiety has been replaced with curiosity.

The difference is I am confident things will be
fine, even though I don't know what shape
they'll take. That's where the curiosity comes
from. Instead of being eaten with fear and
anxiety, I think, 'Oh, hi there, that's
interesting.' I'm not sure where I'll be in a
year but I'm having fun getting there and not
worried. If this doesn't turn out to be what
I'm called to do, something else will show up

and that would be fine too. I have given
myself the gift of some time with less income
and feel everything will work out. I have
purposely turned down more lucrative
consulting jobs where I would have to take
on accountability for what is going to
happen.

Mary agrees she is making choices now based on how they make her feel rather than how much money or status they offer. It's a different standard of measurement, an inner criterion that shapes the options she chooses. In her early sixties, Mary says she has a financial goal but won't sell her soul for external gain anymore. She has suffered some losses along the way. "I hope to repair a friendship that has come apart during my transition. And I have lost my stature as a CEO and the financial security that went with it, although on the up side, I am no longer responsible for anyone other than myself."

Mary reports she has been through the stage in her dark night journey of meeting the Discarded Other. In her case, without hesitation, she says it is her artistic self. "I remember the moment in fourth grade when I created a fantastic snow scene on a piece of black paper using white crayon. I just got lost in that scene. It was beautiful. I was very proud of it. I was so hurt when the teacher gave me a poor grade, I put my artistic self away on that day."

A few years ago, as Mary complained of her boredom, a friend unearthed through a survey process the three areas for Mary to engage in for a satisfying life—artistic, musical and literary. She was surprised! Since then, she has carried this unfulfilled yearning with her. "I was encouraged to read as a child but have not, since that moment in fourth grade, followed any creative pathways in my life."

Mary goes on to say she is finding her backyard garden a new means of creative expression.

As I have thought about claiming my discarded artist, I have spent a huge amount of time daydreaming about my garden. When I felt ready to begin, I took a day off and I went to the local garden center. I love the garden center, my blood pressure drops whenever I visit, and many of the staff know me. This time, though, I didn't ask any of the experts about what to buy or plant. Instead, I wandered around for a couple of hours, I read about the different plants, I talked to them, I connected with their energy. I ended up with a giant basket of plants, needing help

*to get it all to the counter, saying to myself,
'I'll be lucky to get out of here under five
hundred dollars.' The total was just under!*

*I've spent several days planting since
my visit. I've got everything in the ground
and things are coming into bloom. When I
look at my garden now, if I hear a criticism, I
am able to say, 'This is my garden and I'm
going to do it the way I want to.' I don't care
what anyone else thinks about it. That feels
like meeting my discarded artistic self. I'm
honouring and enjoying my lost artist,
claiming her really for the first time.*

Mary says she is experiencing different
behaviour in other areas, too. "I have so much
energy for exploring art in all its forms, with others
and especially on my own. As I take advantage of
these opportunities, there I am, my artistic self!" She
is also beginning to read literature and enjoy it
differently than before. She is listening to various
kinds of music more often, and going to galleries to
study the art. There are also little things. "I'm
bringing cut flowers in from the garden again. My
office is full of artfully arranged peonies at the
moment."

Mary describes adventuring into this new territory as like a meeting with a stranger who inhabits her days, herself but not herself. "I feel I'm still on the verge of discovering who this artistic self is, what her characteristics are, what feeds her. She didn't get to grow up so how do I let her become the adult Mary now? I'm actually feeling shy about it. Is she going to like me? Am I going to like her?" She adds with a chuckle, "Will I end up wearing long flowing skirts and Birkenstocks, let my hair grow and have a ponytail?"

Mary tells me about a dream she had she called "Managing the Whole Room." She is in a room full of women all talking at once, some presenting ideas, others working quietly. She helps a soft-spoken woman by using her loud voice. "There is someone here who wants to be heard. Listen!" The cloth dividing the room in two disappears. She collects colourful candy and adds it to a curved diagram her high school chum is creating.

Reflecting on the dream, Mary says she has mostly demonized her bold self, but she is the one who unites the two sides of her room. "The dream integrates masculine and feminine aspects of me, quiet, studious, smart, soft-spoken, creative and bold. And by the way, I can add colour to a room!" I also notice there is no conflict, judgment or negativity in the dream. It is all about strengths and becoming whole. She is re-creating who she is as she begins to emerge from her time in the Underworld.

She is also remembering her physical body in new ways these days. The work in her garden is much more physically taxing than Mary is used to. Her feet, knees and hips have hurt for years. She has recently recovered from knee surgery and now finds she is capable of kneeling down on the ground and doing the digging, bending and lifting required for gardening.

> *I'm very aware that I am physically capable. Yesterday I worked in the garden, digging up rocks, using a pickaxe, and I was exhausted. Even while I was doing it, I was thinking, 'Am I going to get sick? Am I going to throw up I'm so tired?' I'd get up and go get a bag of soil and realize my back and knees didn't hurt. I was just hot and sweaty. It was a new feeling. I came in and got in the tub, went to bed at nine o'clock, and was completely and utterly satisfied. Today I don't have any sore muscles. I feel very energetic and I'm planning to do more planting.*

This focus on her garden seems a classically feminine way to build a new self, out of the earth, out of generosity of spirit and love of beauty.

The image Mary carries about her journey these days is making her way up a serpentine mountain path. "As I walk, I am hearing new sounds coming across the range, I feel a warm breeze on my skin from the other side, a mixture of air, dry or humid. There are also new smells to take in, and I feel alive."

She pauses in this description to tell me that this is the first spring her garden has a new perfume in it, although she has almost all the same flowers. I suggest she is just noticing it differently—the perfume isn't new, she is!

Mary is also planning on trying creative expression to support her coaching clients in connecting to their authentic selves. She already uses coloured pens and sticky notes to encourage creative expression but wonders about asking clients to bring their favourite art, music, and so on, as part of the process.

At this point, we begin to talk about beauty as perhaps the heart of Mary's dark night story. "When I look at myself in the mirror these days, I say to myself, 'I'm pretty good looking.' Answering the call has enabled me to set aside the negative beliefs about myself." She admits she has spent most of her life feeling "fat and ugly" but is letting go of those judgements. As she reclaims her artistic self, her own lost artist, her beauty, she sees it all around her. The beauty in her garden, in her body, in her coaching, in all the creative avenues she is exploring. Integrative medicine author and teacher Dr. Rachel Naomi Remen says, "At the deepest level, the creative process and the healing process arise from a single source. When you are an artist, you are a healer."[10] I see this in Mary, using her creativity to heal that disappointed child, to give her a new life. And to bring that healing energy to her clients as well.

Stories of Ascent

Donald's Story: The Slender Thread

The deepest trance possible is the one we're already in.
. . . Milton Erickson

At seventy-seven, Donald was broke. He doesn't look the part of the down-and-out cowboy, his long, lanky frame and chiselled good looks exuding elegance and serenity. He surprised everyone who knew him with the revelation that he was running out of money. He had left his orthodontic practice twenty-eight years earlier and bought an eighty-six acre property in the Four Corners area of the south-western US, along the pathways of the ancient Anasazi, Navajo, Hopi and Ute tribes.

He called it Sage Canyon Ranch and built his first home, the Cliff House, extending right out of the red rock. He lived in it for a couple of years. Then, after he sold his ski condo in Purgatory, he built a second, larger ranch house for himself that he could use for clients and workshops in his growing coaching business. He continued to extend the ranch, funding the purchases from his retirement account, until he had added over a hundred acres to the property. His funds were shrinking.

Longtime friends came for extended visits and gradually a permanent community began to grow around Donald and the magic of this sacred land. Friends bought a piece of his land and built their own home. The Cliff House was rented to two couples, the women running vision quest retreats during the summer months. His brother moved onto the property, contributing significantly to the day-to-day running of the ranch. For a time, the community thrived. However, political and social differences with his brother became insurmountable at the time of the 2016 presidential elections and Donald finally asked him to move on. It was a bitter parting, leaving Donald without the help or finances to maintain the ranch. He admits, "The separation with my brother is a big part of things going south for me. It started the ball rolling downhill." The darkness was descending.

Donald put out a call for ideas, revealing his financial crisis, and the community responded. No one wanted to see things change and with the best of intentions, they stepped in to preserve the status quo. His financial situation was analyzed and alternatives for generating funds were considered. His vision had always been to use the ranch to support the evolution of human consciousness. He hoped people would come to the ranch for self-realization, to be healed there as he had been. And they did, but not to the extent needed to sustain his expenditures. The question of selling off pieces of the ranch was raised but everyone hoped another way could be found.

There was also the subtext of how this could have happened. Following surgery for bladder cancer a few years earlier, even Donald felt his capabilities were in question. Describing this sense of loss, he says, "It felt like I was losing my self-sufficiency and independence in this aging process. The ranch holdings were too big, too much work, I was holding on to too much. I had to let go."

This letting go required Donald to trust in an internal strength and acceptance that had eluded him for most of his life. "The fear was that I'd be alone and alienated, not belonging. I had not trusted I was really never alone." He refers to "the slender thread" running throughout his life, that enduring connection he now feels assures belonging. Using his passion for snowboarding as a metaphor, he says, "I can ride the slender thread in life just as I do on the board with the thread of gravity doing the work of keeping me connected to Mother Earth, letting me dance with the snow and build that relationship with her music. I can trust that."

He tells the story of how his insight about trust emerged. He was with his longtime teacher and in a moment of profound appreciation, he said to him through his tears, "I trust you more than I've ever trusted anyone." His teacher cupped his hands around Donald's face, looked him deeply in the eyes and responded, "You know it's not me you trust." Donald says, "It was like a bolt of lightning. I was learning to trust myself and the pull of my curiosity that had brought me to this point in life. I thought about the ceiling in the Sistine Chapel, the finger pointing to divinity. That divinity is in me, not outside of myself. My Discarded Other was trust in myself and it was time to reclaim it."

Donald now uses the phrase "what wants to happen" as a way of trusting the universe in its wisdom, trusting whatever happens in life to guide him, following the thread of his never-ending curiosity to balance life's ups and downs, just as he does on his snowboard. As he ages, he finds his self-importance diminishing, his ego losing the power to feel in control of events. He feels the darkness gathering around him whenever he creates an image of how he needs to be for others or feels that he has to be a certain way to make others happy. He notes, "I changed. I stopped trying to make others happy. I became wise enough to trust

130

just sitting back and listening, not always having something to say. I now allow things to be rather than to think I need to change so much of what happens in life. I trust something much bigger than my ego."

He also speaks about his feminine side, how the slender thread consists of both masculine and feminine.

I have lots of masculine strength, the 'get things done' kind of energy. The feminine is tenderness, kindness, receptivity. This side of me is actually my safe harbour but I have hidden it because I didn't trust it as being enough. I didn't allow myself to be curious about the feminine part of who I am. During this dark process, I had to allow that part to come out, to see it as a strength, an essential piece of wholeness.

Donald sees the ranch as a feminine strength that truly fulfills his need to belong. He remembers sitting on the porch of the Cliff House at sunset, singing out, "My Heart's Found a Home" as loudly as he could. "I gave my feminine a home and she returned it to me."

Rebirth and its sacrifices have come with change at the ranch. Several parcels have been sold and two of his dearest friends have left. In the course of his dark night there have been difficult conversations, criticisms by others of

131

Donald's mercurial personality and ability to make life decisions, the hurtful consequences of his changing plans, of his reckless spending habits concerning the ranch. In his darkest moments, he reflects, "I felt betrayed by my closest friends and it threw me into a spin. I felt deeply troubled and fell into a depression." In the end, just as happened with his brother, separation was again necessary. He says sadly, "I didn't want to drive anyone away, but I needed to trust I knew what kind of help was really helpful as I make end-of-life decisions. I guess it's inevitable that the crowd thins but there is such richness with those who remain."

There are new faces at the ranch. The community is growing with new owners of the parcels Donald has sold in order to fund the rest of his life. "I am mourning the necessary losses—the lost relationships, my lost youth, my diminishing capacities. And I am facing my mortality. If I were flying, I'd be on the final approach, looking for a soft landing." Despite these losses, Donald is upbeat, eloquent, surrendered. "I'm simplifying, getting clear on what's important."

One of the gifts of the dark night journey is this clarity. For Donald, raising consciousness about the unfolding climate crisis has become a priority, living as he does in the high desert where the water is drying up. He has not only simplified his own life and use of resources but has formed a group who meet routinely to discuss action strategies and make recommendations to city council about the threats of climate change to their area. "This is our dark night scenario, that this land will become uninhabitable. We are hiding the dark side, pretending, based on a deep fear, rather than owning it and taking responsibility for it now." This focused energy is indicative of rebirth, of the new meaning and contribution Donald is discovering, the new light out of the darkness.

Sheila's Story: Feeling the Feelings

Surrender is not surrendering to someone or something. It is totally releasing the narrative that has been moving us forward.
. . . Rodney Smith

Sheila is full of energy and enthusiasm, sometimes leaving one idea unfinished to replace it with a better or different one or stopping to laugh or ask a question or check that you're with her in her train of thought. She is engaging and insightful, making her a delight to have a conversation with. Sheila is an Australian living in Sydney. She has co-owned two businesses: a women's adventure travel business and a funky regional arts center. She is currently an Integral Coach and Facilitator and is developing a project to build our human capacity in dealing with wicked problems such as climate change.

Sheila was in her mid-fifties when her dark night began. We have talked about our journeys before, when we were both in the midst of them, so we pick up in the middle of the process by reflecting on how difficult it is to stay centered through the dark depths. She says, "It's not like we're in a monastery where we're being looked after and can focus on contemplative study. How do you stay grounded in that space in a dominant culture where you feel so adrift?" It's a question we'll come back to later in the conversation. Sheila tells me, "I had a fairly rough night which was odd and did make me think of how we can revisit these dark places again and again. It had a quality like cortisol firing and refiring. I was restless. So I'm warmed up!"

When I ask Sheila how her dark night began, she replies, "I was dragged kicking and screaming. When I look back, I realize there were many opportunities to enter through a more gradual doorway, lots of platforms I blithely ignored for years." The event that catalyzed this deep dive into the darkness was the end of initially one and then two relationships, when a former partner began an intimate liaison with Sheila's current partner.

It took some months for the reality to unfold but the journey was a complete mind-bender. It was one of the hardest things I have ever dealt with and one of the worst reactions I have ever experienced. I was devastated by the loss of two such close and once-dear friends.

I began to see that the abandoned one is the core of my makeup. My parents separated when I was five days old. My mum and I went to live with her parents and in a couple of weeks her father dropped dead. My mum lost her milk so I was popped into a care home where in the fifties babies were left to cry until they got over it. My mother said I was a very troubled child and she later became overprotective. I went from abandonment to overbearing mothering, so my early attachment history is very mixed up.

My ears always perk up at childhood abandonment because of my own history, so I asked how she believes it has affected her life.

I spent a lot of my childhood developing as robust an ego as I could. I set up a very strong group of people around me and then I

135

bullied them if they went out of line because
there was no way I was going to be left alone
in that big hall as the only baby in swaddling
just crying my little heart out. So I secured
people at a very young age and kept them
very close to me for a very long time. My
father was a bully as well so I had quite good
role modeling. I had to learn to stand up to
him.

I also learned there are a couple of ways to
get through this. I would be a really high-
performing athlete because if you just win the
race, get all the records, then no one can
accuse you of not being good enough. And I
would get this group of friends around me
who are really solid and I wouldn't let them
break ranks.

Sheila's strategy was highly successful. It wasn't until
she was nineteen that she began to understand her
behaviour. "I was devastated when I started to realize the
extent of my bullying because it hadn't been mirrored back
to me at all. I got away with it for a very long time. What
you don't experience as a child, then when you experience
it as an adult, it's horrible. The ground beneath us is not as
stable as I made my ground."

And so when the relationships with her friends ended and her dark night began, Sheila slowly recognized why her feelings of abandonment were so severe.

That event was the 'kicking and screaming down you go' thing. It did feel like being dragged totally unwillingly on my back by multiple hands not my own into a place where then you're just trapped, there are no doors. I remember how terrifying it was. I was really terrified.

In the deep dark, Sheila had to face her demons: her bullying, her aggressiveness, her "overblown ego" that had been so successful. "That confident capable person had to be recreated through the whole dark night, not forsaking the ego completely but reconstructing her into a healthy performing partner in life." She had to let go of the stability of her carefully constructed self, to mourn her loss of certainty and take off her masks one by one. "It still presents challenges at times." She notes, for example, she's lost the "gift of egoic gab," sometimes having to just notice she is less successful and sit in this different space. "I am mostly OK with it but sometimes it hurts."

Sheila says she spent the better part of three years in the Underworld, at the bottom of a deep well. "I was totally lost. The pain and anguish were resolute. There was nowhere to go. I thought at the time there was nothing here but this miserable sod. I was quite shocked at how little I valued my life. I got stuck there for quite some time."

As we talk, she remembers as a child being very sad and not understanding why. "We were very comfortable and I couldn't reconcile my sadness. My father said 'You're too young to have emotions, children don't have feelings.'" I ask Sheila to tell me more about these feelings of sadness. I wonder if we are coming to the Discarded Other in her story.

"I had spent a lifetime denying feelings, I squashed my feelings. In the person I had constructed there was no room for feelings. The bully didn't have feelings, she engendered them in others." Reclaiming her feelings was a rebirth for Sheila but required enormous inner work. She had psychotherapy to get in touch with her feelings but then had to figure out what to do with them.

> *I was doing Feelings 101 in my fifties! I spent six to nine months dealing with all the feelings backed up at the door. I had to work through all of them. It was like ten thousand debtors had come to collect. I had to feel each of them, contextualize them, say I was sorry. I had to re-journey that, all pushing in me to get air space.*

I ask what helped and Sheila lists several things. She found that astrology gave her a context, a way to imagine the possibility of change in her circumstances. And she had three superb friends who stuck with her even when, as she notes, "I got concerned, people were so bored with me." The best resource, however, was an online program called *Willing to Feel*. "The icing on the cake was Diane Hamilton's program. She explains the process of working through feelings. It blew me away. It's simple and I use it still."

We return to the question of staying grounded when you're feeling adrift. Sheila says one of her sacrifices as she has moved out of the darkness is losing her tribe, her former close connections that now seem out of place, that don't feel like home anymore.

> *It was a huge sacrifice to see myself not as a well-established popular person. I've become a marginal person in my own city where I've been comfortable and confident. I totally lost place and still have, really. I'm only grounded through myself now, not through those connections. Where my outriggers were firmly placed in a whole lot of other groups and people, like little spider legs, I had to*

retract those and do my own housekeeping completely.

Sheila has noticed that she wants a wider tribe, a global network, more diverse connections. We agree that it seems the more we broaden our horizons, the more we must rely on ourselves, on nourishing and nurturing both the breadth and the depth.

As we come to the gifts Sheila has received from her dark night journey and how she will take those into the world, she impresses me with an idea that has stayed with me since we talked.

I'd love to see a dark night network really build up capacity to hold people through it, from a wisdom and compassion point of view. I don't feel skilled up to play that role but for the planet and our society I want to be much stronger in that foundation and in our network and much more able to offer help.

It doesn't feel fleshed out yet but we know a web of connectivity is essential. The people who showed up for us in our dark night, we'll never forget them. And they didn't need to do much, they just needed to be prepared to listen again or to be with you when you're a

mangled mess. My hope is that we can build
capacity in this area and offer something
perhaps for individuals but also for groups.

We ended the conversation with Sheila summarizing her dark night. "Waking up to the fact that I'm a highly sensitive little being with deep feelings is a gift. It connects into my childhood story and points me toward the future."

These stories are all about coming to wholeness, of reclaiming that discarded inner part of ourselves we have lost along the way. They are stories of both despair and hope, darkness and light, the coming together of our opposites in a new harmony. For me, they are representative of the imbalance of masculine over feminine expression in our culture and the personal journeys courageous men and women are taking to create coherence in themselves and in our world.

[6] Fischer, Angela. "Entering the Secret," in *The Unknown She: Eight Faces of an emerging consciousness,* edited by Hilary Hart (Inverness CA: The Golden Sufi Center, 2004), 30.

[7] Kramer, Kenneth. *Redeeming Time: T.S. Eliot's Four Quartets* (Cambridge MA: Cowley Publications, 2007), 174.

[8] Meredith, Jane. *Journey to the Dark Goddess: How to return to your soul* (Washington DC: Moon Books, 2011), 4.

[9] Bolen, Jean Shinoida. *Goddesses in Older Women: Archetypes in women over fifty* (New York: Harper, 2014), 63.

[10] Remen, Rachel Naomi. *Kitchen Table Wisdom: Stories that heal* (New York: Penguin, 2006), 146.

PART THREE:

ACCOMPLISHING THE PASSAGE

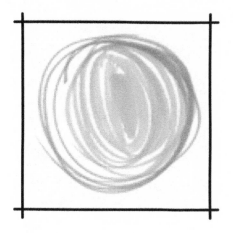

Chapter Five
Themes in the Dark Night Journey

Neither ego nor shadow can be redeemed unless its twin is transformed. It is this rubbing together that brings them both back to their original wholeness.
. . . Robert A. Johnson

The overarching theme I have identified is reclaiming the feminine or some aspect of feminine qualities that have been diminished in our current culture. This is arising now because we are both individually and culturally out of balance and in need of psychic healing, of reconciling the masculine and feminine poles, and bringing feminine values to the fore for the sake of the world. These values can vary but tend to center on feeling as well as thinking, receiving as well as giving, loving ourselves as well as others, attending to the creative as well as the rational, the spiritual as well as material.

Related to this overarching reclaiming of the feminine are a dozen themes that have emerged both from my own experience of my dark night and conversations with others undergoing and analyzing their own journeys. Each person engaged in a dark night will experience some, although perhaps not all, of the themes at some point in the process. I have described them below in a loose association with the stages in the passage, but this ordering, like the stages themselves, should not be taken as linear—a particular theme can show up any time during the dark night, or not at all.

The twelve themes are as follows:

- Inward-turning
- Questioning
- Discontinuity
- Shadow Work
- Revelations
- Dreams

- Attachments
- Support
- Images and Metaphors
- Death
- Transformation
- Mystical Mysteries

Inward-turning

It is natural to become more reflective as we age. It is one of the hallmarks of maturity, at whatever age, to become oriented toward our inner life as well as our outer circumstances. We become increasingly reflective, find solace in introspection, perhaps turn our attention to a mindfulness practice or contemplative path. Some of this quieting down may be physically driven. We find we have less energy for being on the go all the time. We begin to value stillness and settling. To the young, this may look like the stereotypical cardigan and slippers but as we mature, it is simply beginning to recognize the merits of being rather than doing. Emotionally, there may be less need for drama as our store of experiences teaches us that life is full of ups and downs.

As we become more reflective, we may realize there is a vast territory, sometimes completely undiscovered, that awaits within. We can explore this territory through meditation or contemplation, or we can be forced to confront it through losses and disappointments. Either way, we find ourselves questioning, digging into our awareness, foraging among our memories for answers to the most fundamental life enquiries: Who am I? What is my purpose here? How have I done so far? The choice we face is either to turn away, to ignore the call and live in the disquiet of our familiar outward life as long as we can, or to turn toward the unknown landscape and dare to enter.

In my case, it wasn't until I became exhausted and disillusioned with corporate and university life that I realized that my intellectual development was no longer effective, because the corresponding emotional development had not taken place. On the masculine/feminine continuum, I was heavily polished on the masculine elements and very scruffy on the feminine ones. It was clearly time for evening up.

Nadine's story of letting go is similar, being addicted to work most of her life, ignoring her inner self until the third of three calls pushed her over the threshold into her dark night. Nadine felt that the quiet time, the loss of self, allowed her to see the magic in the darkness. She says, "It's all there already but it's a question of where you're looking and trusting that the inner mystery is unfolding."

Donald speaks of getting in touch with his inner trust in what wants to happen as a result of the dark time he has been through. "Sometimes when I needed to speak, I didn't. I didn't trust myself. I have changed. I've stopped being nice to make others happy. I trust my intuition in the moment." As he moves toward his eighties, he finds his self-importance diminishing, his ego relinquishing its control.

Charlotte, with her many losses, has been forced to turn inward by circumstances in her life, the loss of friends and family, and her sense of belonging. "I feel like I've been in this pit for a long time." For solace, Charlotte turns to nature, to her garden and her memories of times past.

Questioning

If we choose to explore this inner terrain, we are on the brink of the dark night. We can of course, at least for a time, turn back, decide it's just navel gazing, and get on with life. But if we heed the call and have the courage, we enter a period where we question everything and see that what we have believed has been largely mistaken. Einstein called this kind of discovery an "optical delusion".

We find discontinuities, incongruities, in everything we turn our attention to: our work, our families, our life choices. We surface our regrets, our mistakes, our harsh or hasty decisions and their consequences. We question, question, question. We may find ourselves with pieces of what we thought was our successful life scattered on the ground. It is a successful life, isn't it? Everything I've worked for is worth it, isn't it? I've spent my life energy on the right things, right? What are the right things? Am I happy? Am I fulfilled? If I died tomorrow, would I feel I have lived the life I wanted?

As the questions come and the answers are not resoundingly positive, there is a growing gap between the inner and outer worlds. This gap is an entry portal into the dark night journey. It has been referred to as "the cloud of unknowing," a mystifying fog that descends to burden our thoughts and emotions, drain our energy and leave us wandering in the twilight.

My cloud of unknowing was about my lifestyle. I enjoyed fifteen years of being a gypsy vagabond, travelling the world for work and pleasure, being constantly on the go and loving the excitement and adventure of it all. Then a slowly growing pall fell over my joy. What I imagined was stepping back, settling down, and staying in one place for a while. I yearned for an ordinary life, although I had no idea

149

what that meant. It raised endless questions about every aspect of my life, none of which I could answer.

Mary has had similar lifestyle questions as she reconnects with her discarded artistic self. It is such unfamiliar territory that she has had to question everything about what life will be like with this new outlook. A whole world of possibilities has opened up. She laughs, "Should I get the nose ring? Should I buy the RV and move to Colorado?"

Dirk, in the deep dark night, is questioning what his life will be like after his stroke. He is struggling to answer the questions "Why me? Why now?" He comments that he has asked himself many times why he meditates and now sees it has given him "a spark of hope" even when he has felt quite bitter. "I have asked myself what I would have expected it to be like and I think it could have been much worse. Through meditation, I am able to be aware and conscious of what is happening and live through it."

Discontinuity

Dark nights are characterized by discontinuity; that is their nature. As soon as we stop questioning because we have come upon a solution, there is a sheer, the kind of free-fall drop you feel when an airplane hits turbulence. Something else is going on.

One of the common discontinuities is finding a window in the tunnel and breathing in the momentary light, perhaps even believing it's over, until we drop back into the blackness once more. We might wake up one morning, feel good and sense the fog has lifted, our world is clear and certain once again. For a time, it is as though it was just a bad dream, a temporary blip in our otherwise fairly satisfactory lives. We get on with the business of living, glad to have that, whatever it was, behind us. These moments of reprieve can last anywhere from days to months but just as soon as we are sure it is over, it is not. We are plunged back into the dark night with a force often even more powerful than before.

The dark night is therefore best seen as a cycling of darkness and light rather than a continuous unidirectional process, both in its overall shape and in its component parts. As we navigate the passage, these respites of lightness may be required for regaining our sense of equilibrium, integrating what we have learned so far, and gathering our courage for the continuing journey. The cycles may also simply be our resistance to the journey, wanting to take a break from the turmoil. The number of cycles will vary according to the person's appetite for the work. Even when the dark night is over and the light shines through, there are always these cycles, perhaps not as deep or dire, once we are awake to both the darkness and the light of life.

Sheila speaks of this temporary respite that lulls us into thinking we are through the dark. "I often remember that sense of getting one foothold, or one reprieve, or one insight and you'd think, 'Oh great, there is some light up there' and you'd crane your neck and you'd see a tiny speck and then before you knew it, the foothold broke and down you went." The sense of loss of the familiar foundations of our lives through surprise circumstances, the discontinuities we can't predict or control, can be very unsettling.

For me, the solution seemed to be finding a home, a haven filled with beauty, harmony and love. But each time I tried, I found the opposite—a place of conflict, disharmony and suffering. Three times I repeated the process; three times I created a new external place in search of inner peace. And got the same result each time. It was the definition of insanity, doing the same thing over and over again, expecting different results! The discontinuity between my inner and outer worlds was obvious, but it took me a long time and a lot of resistance before I recognized it.

Nadine had a similar pattern of moving across Canada and back and forth to New Zealand in search of a place of peace she could call home. Each time she did, a cycle of disastrous events followed, sapping her energy.

"Then the fear started. I am a walking disaster, I have no resilience left at this point, I don't even know if I can hold myself together." The discontinuities kept coming.

Shadow Work

The hardest work of the dark night is confronting our shadow side, those parts of ourselves that we have avoided, buried in our depths where we can't see them, but that have nonetheless continually influenced our behaviour. These qualities are like heavy stones we haul around in a large bag, pretending it's not there while it drags us down, hampering our freedom. Others, especially those close to us, can see these qualities in our personality quite clearly, although we do not. And we often project our shadows outward onto others rather than admitting them to ourselves. Why is he so judgmental? How can she be so vain? These questions, when turned around to face in our own direction, are often the clues to our own shadows, the qualities in ourselves we dare not let into the light.

As we descend into the darkness, we must peel back these layers of self-deception to disclose our naked humanity: the good and bad, our pride and shame, our arrogance and carelessness, whatever lurks beyond our notice. This process, too, happens in cycles of discovery as we shine the light on one negative aspect of ourselves and

153

are shocked by its truth, only to find that it is one of many demons we have stored down in the dungeons of our unconscious. Bringing them up into the light of consciousness is our only option for maturation but it takes time, effort and courage.

One of these moments for me was my brief foray back into university teaching, a place I was at home, where I had been successful. I was pretty sure I had done my shadow work; I had been at it for years and thought I knew myself well. My pride in my abilities and my arrogance about my success were the obvious clues but I missed them in my zeal to avoid looking at these truths. I had to turn the camera around to look plainly at my own self-righteousness, my conceit. How the mighty fall!

Our deepest demons are the ones that plague us repeatedly until we can turn to face them, to open that dread-filled door to our darkest secrets. We may get only a hint of them unless we are willing to plumb the depths of our unconscious, but the signs will be everywhere. And the harder we resist looking, the stronger the clues become.

At the core of this shadow process we finally find the innermost darkness in ourselves, the quality we have abandoned, thrust aside as a defect, our Discarded Other. This is the moment of truth in the dark night journey. Sheila had to reclaim her discarded feelings, for example, the deeply buried and protected emotions she had covered over since childhood by being a bully. Being in the deep dark with all these cast-off feelings took tremendous effort and courage. "People saw me living the dream and it was a nightmare!"

Revelations

The gold in this difficult shadow work is the gift of insight, understanding, self-knowledge and maturity. Our introspection leads eventually to revelation and with it comes a new freedom and lightness we have not known before. We become more integrated human beings, more aware of who we are, for better and worse. Based on these revelations we can now make corrections, change our ways, and seek forgiveness where necessary. In the end, this forgiveness must extend to ourselves and this can be the toughest turn of all. Acknowledging our weaknesses and imperfections with acceptance—even seeing them as gifts of understanding, not only of our own but others' weaknesses—we can become more compassionate humans in the world.

Through the long dark night, the revelations come. They can wash over us unexpectedly with a kind of knowing we have not experienced before. If we have a daily practice of meditation, journaling or just stillness, these little nuggets will be revealed in their own time. They may not make a lot of sense or fit together in any meaningful way. They are just insights about us, about life, to be acknowledged and perhaps explored further. They always seem to bring with them a lightness, a smile, a quiet aha, a wonderment, a tear. In the midst of our turmoil we have little capacity yet to integrate these revelations into our lives. They are just accumulating treasures, like stars in the night sky that light our way along the road.

I had a number of these revelations during the long years of my dark night. One I particularly remember occurred early on when I had been meditating for about six months. I was using Michael Brown's *The Presence Process* and its six-word mantra, "I am here now in this." I enjoyed playing with it to suit my mood and current circumstances, like "I am here now in bliss" or "I am nowhere in this." One morning in the midst of trying to still my mind, I was bathed in a message that said, "I have been here forever." It was me saying it to myself and yet it wasn't me at all—I had never had that thought before. And the feeling that washed over me was of such peace and spaciousness that it took me several moments to comprehend, even a little, what had happened. I could only think of it as some kind of mystical download, a different kind of knowing, one I have experienced many times over the succeeding years.

Nadine had several of these mysterious downloads early in her dark night, first the invocation to "Get on your bike and ride," and then to, "Fire yourself." Another was the strong sense she should sell her house. Nadine followed these injunctions as they led her deeper into her journey, into herself and the further realizations that awaited her.

Donald had a powerful revelation when he emotionally told his longtime teacher how much he trusted him, and the teacher replied, "You know it's not me you trust." Donald realized with a shock that he needed to trust his instincts, his curiosity, his own divinity. Similarly, after years of wondering why he meditated, Dirk realized It has given him "a spark of hope" even when he has felt quite bitter. "It could have been much worse. Through meditation, I am able to be aware of what is happening and live through it."

Dreams

Many dark night journeys involve unusual dreams. Dreams are our window into the unconscious and are therefore another resource for revealing what is in the shadows. They are an additional gold mine to explore in the dark night. Often what we dare not bring to the surface during our waking hours will emerge during our dreams as images, scenes and creations relating to our depths. Many of us say we cannot remember our dreams but keeping a dream journal and recording even the smallest snippets will, over time, allow us to recall more of our dream time and its subterranean interpretive material.

Our dreams can bring new insights and perspectives about what is happening in our daily lives. They can be positive and helpful. Mary, for example, had a dream that seemed to highlight her talents and qualities, even her bold self she had kept under wraps. In it, she adds colour to the space and tells herself, "There is someone here who wants to be heard. Listen!" This dream gave her confidence for moving through her dark night.

Dreams can, on the other hand, awaken deep fears and dreads as well as our own demonic natures. These nightmares can include horrors of every kind and can be very disturbing. They will not necessarily occur in a dark night passage but if they do, it is important to know that they are a normal part of unearthing all of who we are. I had several such nightmares. The monstrous demons in our unconscious—the rage, terror, hatred, and savagery—are there in each of us. These primitive forces, when hidden, can be activated in our judgements and behaviour toward others. They can also show up in the collective unconscious without our realizing it and can lead to social injustice.

Once owned, these forces are less likely to come into play without our knowledge.

Dreams were so important to Freud that he called them the "royal road" to the unconscious, conveying messages from the deep parts of the self.

Attachments

As we sink into the dark night, we may have several false starts or distractions where we believe we can either avoid or overcome the darkness with some new activity or opportunity that presents itself, or by grinding away at some status quo we are not yet willing to give up. These attachments usually serve only to deepen our alienation. As the Borg in *Star Trek* say: "Resistance is futile."

Our attachments ground us in our worlds, connect us to ourselves and each other, and confirm for us that we are important. They are also the ropes that bind us to our current reality, our usual ways of making meaning. Dark nights are designed to break these ropes, to tear down the identity we are attached to, and with it sometimes to destroy our whole world as we know it. Dark nights pull the comfortable turf out from under us so we can eventually stand on higher ground.

We can try to short-circuit this process by looking for shortcuts and half measures that may get us through the night unscathed, or so we think. But resistance only steepens our descent. Instead of potentially having some say in our route to the bottom, we may be pushed over the edge by life circumstance: illness, loss, hardship. In the words of the old Zen proverb, "Let go or be dragged." Unfortunately, there are no shortcuts.

This is equally true of the ascent, when the worst of the darkness has faded and we feel ourselves rising into a new world. It is so tempting to race through it. It's been dark for so long and the light is so appealing. But a slow ascent is necessary to recreate who we are becoming and to take the care required for the full blossoming of our new identity. Too quick reattachments will short-circuit this process and cripple the fragile imago emerging from the cocoon.

When we finally let go of our previous attachments, it can feel like a significant loss. Sheila, for example, talks of losing her close connections that no longer seemed to fit who she was becoming. She has had to detach from her previous relationships that tethered her to outdated ways of thinking. "I had to let go of my tribe even though I still look for them and I yearn for them." Mary speaks of losing her stature as CEO and the financial security that went with it. She has had to give herself permission to follow "an inner criterion" that shapes the options she chooses, even though there are still moments of fear.

Dirk's letting go of his attachment to his physical capabilities is ongoing. He is confronting a major change in his lifestyle and identity as a result of his stroke. He realizes, "The darkness is holding me where I am." Charlotte is questioning many of her previous attachments and feeling that she doesn't fit in anywhere. One of them is her long attachment to the Quakers because of her father's being "the embodiment of a Quaker." She is now beginning to realize that she doesn't belong in the community and it doesn't bring her joy. What should she do? "Sometimes it feels like a complete loss of faith."

Support

The role of others in our journey through the dark night is critically important every step of the way. Not to travel beside us, for that would accomplish little, but to be a witness to our transformation, to see us and know us along the way even when we ourselves are totally lost. The ones who hold a candle in the wind light our way just enough to keep us going, to reassure us that we are here and we are valued. They are a lifeline to normality. They may show up as mentors, guides, or supporters of all kinds in many different ways. Their role might be a coach, a chaplain, a therapist, or a close friend. We can also draw on art, poetry, books—anything that feeds our need for connection when we are feeling alienated from life.

Mary has found support in her garden, where she is discovering her discarded artistic self among her plantings. "I'm allowing myself to enjoy art and finding opportunities present themselves around me." Her art and artist are new means of connection and expression. Nadine and Charlotte talk about finding new friends unexpectedly. Nadine talks about many friends showing up at just the right time. "It was such a surprise . . . it seemed like a miracle."

Our guides may not always be obvious, so it is important to be open to surprises. Children are great supporters of our process without ever knowing it. They can pull us out of our thick stew and into play, laughter, and lightness that brightens the spirits every time. Nature is a wonderful guide too, offering us just the right breeze, slant of the sun, or rustling of the trees to remind us that we are part of everything and cannot be otherwise. Sometimes in conversation, if we mention we are experiencing a dark night, we may find ourselves in deep dialogue with another who has similar thoughts and experiences that are helpful and affirming to share, kindred spirits on the trail.

However, not everyone is an appropriate companion. There may be those close to us who would rather we didn't change so they wouldn't have to change either. Or there may be those who encourage us to move on, to "get over it and get on with it" when that is counterproductive to our dark night process. Or those who would like to give advice or unduly influence our direction. Setting healthy boundaries ensures that we can travel independently and interdependently with others.

For example, Donald has suffered the loss of several of his closest friends with the breakdown in relationships at the ranch when he had to decide what was helpful to him as he prepares for the end of his life.

Images and Metaphors

Unique to each journey yet common in their occurrence are the images or symbols, what British psychoanalyst Donald Winnicott calls "transitional objects," that help us make meaning of what is happening. When we are young, these objects provide the safety we need, like a favourite old blanket or stuffed animal we can't do without. As adults, we can call upon these same objects when we are feeling confused or uncertain, although they may be subtler or more abstract, coming to us in the form of images, symbols and metaphors. They connect us to a language beyond words when we don't yet have the words to describe our experience. They help us to anchor ourselves in more familiar soil. They are, in a sense, guides of a different kind, witnessing our passage and supporting us in holding our centers when we feel in crisis.

These symbols can come from anywhere and can surprise us when they appear. They are at times called totems or spirit guides. We can choose them, or they can choose us. There is something about our chosen symbols that adds meaning or value to our journey, something in their characters we aspire to, perhaps their strength or grace. They can appear in concrete form in our lives as well. These synchronicities mysteriously match the internal images arising from our psyche with the external events happening around us. Although we may approach the whole image idea with a skeptic's questioning, if we are open to the real and symbolic clues that appear throughout the transition, there will be numerous times, too many for disbelief, where we are given concrete demonstrations of the power of this mystery.

One example was my encounter with my turtle guide. I had always had an affinity with turtles, had admired them for being both physically and metaphorically at home, and collected images of them in many shapes and sizes over the years. At one point deep in my dark night I went to Kauai to see the giant sea turtles. It was one of those callings that seemed silly, but it was my birthday. As it turned out, a storm had driven the large turtles out to sea and sure

164

enough, for a week there were none. I was deeply disappointed. Then, while I was snorkeling right at the shore on the final morning, a giant sea turtle swam up behind me out of nowhere, glided quietly just inches under my astonished body, and slowly floated ahead of me, beckoning me to follow. I was spellbound by its fluid beauty. I can't say definitively that it came to find me, but it certainly felt that way, and gave me renewed respect for the mysteries of the path I was on.

Metaphors, like symbols, can also be important because they are an initial framing of an identity we can't now name—a likeness, a draft, when the ultimate shape and details are not yet known. Our psyche often speaks to us in the language of metaphors.

Sheila brings in the metaphor of the darkness as "a relic museum" where our long-forgotten shadows sit waiting in the gloom for us to dig them up. She also refers to the discarded feelings in the museum as "debtors at the door" of her consciousness, waiting to be paid attention. "I had to feel each of them, contextualize them, say I was sorry."

An additional aspect of metaphors is that they are applicable from several points of view. Donald, for example, uses the metaphor of "the slender thread" in a number of ways. He sees it as the connecting filament that assures belonging. "The slender thread is what we all have in common." He also speaks of "riding the slender thread" when he's snowboarding, letting gravity do the work while he dances with the snow. And as he becomes more a witness to being human, he says he is becoming that slender thread himself.

I found the metaphor of a garden very helpful along the way. My role was to tend it and to pass it on fruitfully to the next generation as others had done before me. Mary has also used her garden as a way of getting in touch with her inner artist, using her time choosing plants and then putting them in the ground as a way of getting to know her new self. The image she carries is making her way up a serpentine mountain path, using all of her different senses as she climbs. "It's not terribly strenuous and I am going in the right direction even though I can't see the top . . . my senses are all awake as I move along." Again, if we are open to receiving these images, symbols, and metaphors as they arise, they will bring gifts of understanding out of the disorientation.

Death

A dark night is a death. Andrew Harvey in his memoir *Sun at Midnight,* says, "True rebirth can only come about through a death, the death of the Dark Night; there is no other way."[11] This is one of the most common metaphors, showing up for most of us at some point in our transit through the blackness. It is a death in the sense that we are leaving behind who we were and becoming someone else, we know not who. Life as we have known it is over and what is to come cannot be discerned.

It is not surprising, then, that we mourn our lost life—that familiar, comfortable (if not fully satisfactory) state of affairs. Feelings of loss are a substantial part of the dark night journey. Although a dark night can be depressing, there are rarely thoughts of suicide or prolonged withdrawals from daily tasks. More widespread are feelings of ennui, lethargy, tedium, sadness or melancholy. We walk through our days but not with the usual spring in our step, more like ghosts whose bodies have remained but whose essence has moved on. Those close to us may wonder what has come over us. We may seem distracted, preoccupied and unavailable.

Charlotte is in the midst of this deep grief, what she describes as "the terminal nature of life," with the loss of many friends as well as her sense of belonging. She is dying to what was and not yet clear on the way forward, in a deep well of mourning. Donald is also grieving. "I am mourning the necessary losses, the lost relationships, my lost youth, my diminishing capacities."

Donald alludes here to confronting our own mortality, the fact that we will die, and that we are dying, physically and mentally, as we age. We may feel the loss of vitality and full health, as has happened to Dirk with his stroke. We may experience the deaths of loved ones and suffer the anticipatory grief of the losses to come.

Acknowledging the fragility of life is part of the dying process. Nothing lasts forever, and we are not immortal or indestructible, as many of us have deceived ourselves to be.

Transformation

Through the dark night we experience a developmental transition from one life stage to the next, a taking apart and reassembling of our core beliefs, values and behaviour. It is an evolutionary leap in consciousness, transformation from our current self into a more expansive awareness.

We are evolving beings. We have emerged over fourteen billion years from the stardust of the big bang. What an incredible thought! And we similarly evolve throughout our lifetime, in incremental steps and transcendent leaps, each life a unique contributory flake in cosmic time. We know how to evolve, although we may not know that we know or may resist doing what is necessary, especially as we mature into the higher levels of consciousness and can intuit some of the implications of the journey for us and those around us.

But as we turn inward, we become conscious of our consciousness. We see ourselves from the inside out, noticing we are actually looking through the filters of our minds and hearts out into the world: mediating, judging, interpreting, analyzing, feeling what is out there from in here in the meaning-making process. We become aware of an essence, the consciousness who is doing the looking, who is simply there. We often find this consciousness of a deeper psyche, witnessing everything we experience as we come and go, through quiet, silence, meditation, or reflective contemplation. When we connect with this deeper inner self through our dark night journey it gives us an unchanging stability, a continuing quiet presence beyond our busy minds that is a balm for our disrupted spirit.

Nadine refers to the shift she has experienced as learning to be rather than do. "I think it's about lightness, playfulness, freedom, a sense of connection." She goes on to say, "this is an inner place I feel at home, some familiarity and peace, both internally and in relation to the exterior world, in a very different way than I've ever experienced before."

It is as if that essential or true self is standing back behind layers of curtains that veil what we see in the different shades of our experience. Some of these veils may be transparent, allowing our inner light to authentically shine through. Others may be translucent, allowing some light but dimming our brightness. Then there are the blackout curtains that shut out our light entirely. These are the focus of our transformative darkness, the qualities we are not even aware of that we keep closed from view. Peeling the dark veils from these drapes so they genuinely glisten is the shadow work of the journey. Each individual must come to terms with these blackout curtains and meet the Discarded Other who awaits in the shadows. Transformation is allowing our true brilliance, our whole self in all its aspects, to shine through.

Mary demonstrates this transformation in her discovery of her own beauty, in her garden, in her body, in her coaching, in all the creative avenues she is exploring. She says she is herself but not herself, a transcendent description if ever there was one! Sheila sees her dark night as waking up from a lifetime of denying her feelings. For Charlotte, with all her losses, there are just beginning to be clues to the passage. "It may be something about a transformation from an active external world into a rich and meaningful internal world, the world of experience, imagination and contemplation."

Mystical Mysteries

The final common element in many dark night journeys are mystical mysteries, a connection with the ancient mystical power of evolutionary processes as old as time. Rites of passage have been recognized and ritualized in all cultures through the ages as fundamental turning points in our lives. They have marked the transitions from adolescence to adulthood, from adulthood to elderhood, and from elderhood to death with mystical celebrations and mythological wisdom.

Your particular mysteries will be your own, unlike anyone else's, so it is impossible to say how they will show up. It is only important to be on the lookout for them, to be amazed when they occur, and to learn from them what it is they are here to teach us. If we can approach the journey with some respect for this kind of mystery and for processes we cannot fathom, we may discover that there are many clues, guides and supports awaiting us. We must look to what Jung calls "the trembling edge of our awareness."

Today, we have little time for ritual passages and magical invocations. As our society becomes more material and secular, we hardly acknowledge our turning points, let alone invoke mystical ceremonies or attend to the unseen forces at play. Carol Pearson writes, "It is certainly the lack of such rituals and the relative lack of regard for the spiritual dimension in modern secular society that make these passages so difficult and lonely."[12] As we move into this world of darkness, there are different dynamics to notice. These transition processes are characterized by synchronicities, ironies, paradoxes and serendipity.

When we begin to pay attention to the invisible, the intangible, the ethereal, it is difficult not to associate our experience with mystical, almost magical, synchronicities. A new presence begins to inhabit our lives. We can choose to call it many things depending on our orientation—Self, Spirit, Source, Other, The One, or refer to religious deities—but whatever the term, or no term at all, there is an ineffable dimension, a sense of unity, wholeness, an expanded view we can see into, although perhaps not understand or give credit to initially.

Transpersonal psychologist Stan Grof notes, "Ineffability is a very characteristic feature of mystical states. It is virtually impossible to describe to others the nature of these experiences, their profound meaning, and their significance, particularly to those who have never had them."[13] It is an awakening into a kind of grace, the acceptance of what comes, knowing that we understand so little of the dynamics of our mysterious universe.

For me, there were many of these magical occasions in my dark night years. One quite late in my journey was at a retreat in Santa Fe, where I had focused on my relationship with my mother. We were sitting in our final circle, each taking our turn to offer our last thoughts. It came the turn of the woman next to me, whom I hardly knew except for our few pleasantries through the week. She told of a poem her father had loved and read on significant family occasions. She hadn't thought about it for a long time, but it had come to her and she wondered if she might recite it for us. She began, "My fairest child, I have no song to give you/ No lark could pipe to skies so dull and gray." I drew in my breath, shocked that the poem was the same one my mother had left me on the back of my photograph! How was it possible that this obscure poem written almost two hundred years ago would be spoken now, here in the room? Yet here it was. I felt an intense wave of warmth, love, and connection wash over me as she said the lines, ending with the familiar "One sweet song."

These themes are a beginning. They are the notes I hear as I listen to the dark night song, a discordant refrain of disintegration eventually rising to a melody of wholeness.

[11] Harvey, Andrew. *The Sun at Midnight: A memoir of the dark night* (New York: Tarcher, 2002), 43.

[12] Pearson, Carol. *Awakening the Heroes Within: Twelve archetypes to help us find ourselves and transform our world* (New York: Harper, 1991), 39.

[13] Grof, *The Stormy Search for the Self*, 76.

Chapter Six
Navigating a Dark Night Passage

While waiting for revelation, we do the next right thing. We tell the truth. We do the smallest, realest, most human things. We water that which is dry.
. . . Anne Lamott

A Coaching Perspective

Several of the dark night stories in this book have mentioned the importance of having a coach, therapist, or close friend to witness this difficult time and support the passage by being there. This trusted person would listen intently, might ask a question or two, not judging but understanding, not advising but encouraging, not pushing or pulling but grounded in the current moment, whatever that entails. He or she might suggest a few options but would not be attached to any of them. The few friends who were with me through my journey in this way were invaluable and I will be forever grateful for their presence. So as a coach, I ask myself a question: if I were coaching myself through a dark night, knowing what I now know, how would that look?

This chapter gives you what you need to be your own coach as you venture through your dark night. I have

175

begun with how you may feel at each of the stages. These qualities may act as a diagnostic tool if you are not sure where to put yourself on the dark night map. There are challenges at each of the stages, too, and I have included some of them as examples of what you might be experiencing.

The questions posed for each phase are designed to prompt your thinking and perhaps your writing about your current state, aiming to get at the fundamental issues that arise—not necessarily to find the answers but rather to contribute to your introspection. You might want to have a friend ask you the questions and listen to your answers. Sometimes, giving voice to your thoughts and feelings allows you to see yourself more clearly and gives another person the chance to affirm your experience by feeding it back to you. Or, if you are not ready to engage with another person, you can make a recording of yourself talking through the questions and then play it back, listening for clues or insights in what you are saying.

I have also provided some guidance for what may be helpful to consider at each stage. Any of these ways of navigating your dark night may be helpful in the journey. It is a question of feeling your way into them to see which ones are appropriate to your current circumstances. The journey is a long road and what works now might not work next week, month or year. Ideas you thought wouldn't work for you may come into focus later on. Most of these considerations could be repeated throughout the dark night and they can all be picked up or set down as your needs change. In the deep darkness, it may feel arduous to do anything at all. When you are ready, these prompts may assist in letting go and moving on. Remember, a dark night is not nearly as neat and tidy as it looks in print. It's a messy process!

Navigating Your Descent

The Call from the Psyche

This stage is characterized by confusion, fog, lack of direction, restlessness, alienation from activities, uncertainty about the future, and feeling unsettled or uneasy. One of the challenges is recognizing that this is not business as usual, that something unprecedented is going on. You may hear the call but resist it, trying to figure out your problems in the usual ways rather than acknowledging your bewilderment.

This is a good time to ask yourself how you are feeling, to name your emotional state. What are the circumstances in your life right now that might be contributing to this state? You might also want to ask in what ways this might be the end of a life chapter and the beginning of a transition, and how it may feel both similar to and different from other life chapter endings you've experienced.

Here are five coaching tips related to The Call from the Psyche that may guide you in navigating this stage.

<u>ACCEPTANCE.</u> Accepting that you are in a transition, a transformation of your very self, is one of the challenges that recurs all along the path but is especially difficult when your deep yearning begins to invade your life. You may resist the call for some time, as I did, or eventually be dragged kicking and screaming as Sheila was, or respond only after your ability to resist simply gets worn down, as happened to Nadine. You may also be plunged into a dark night suddenly against your will as Dirk was, fighting for scraps of your former equilibrium. The sooner you acknowledge that this isn't business as usual, the better. You can then stop fighting a losing battle and simply show up, awake and aware, for what wants to happen. Easier said than done, absolutely! But the more you struggle for control and the return to normal, the longer the journey and the deeper your confusion and frustration. You could be stuck for long periods of time in this dark territory. Acceptance is the doorway.

<u>MINDFULNESS.</u> Being mindful is a way of separating the voice in your head, the mind's chatter and struggle, from the

consciousness that notices that voice and can witness it without letting it overwhelm you and become who you are. Mindfulness is just being, letting thoughts rise and fall without feeling the need to do anything about them. Consciousness is the witness of the coming and going. Be that consciousness and watch what happens.

As Michael Singer says in *The Surrender Experiment,* "don't touch it." Just let the reaction, the judgment, the opinion, be there and notice it. Be curious about it, but don't get attached to it. See it as part of your unfolding story, like the other stories in this book. Write it, dance it, sing it, see the themes emerging in your particular journey and notice how they affect you.

SILENCE. How often do you get to hear silence? Our world is so full of noise and activity that we stop noticing the cacophony and chaos around us. Music is pumped into us everywhere: in restaurants, elevators, grocery stores, and medical offices. Television is endemic to Western culture and is often the surround sound to home life. In urban centers, traffic and street noise are continuous. When you are feeling bewildered or anxious, noise simply amplifies the tension.

Silence, on the other hand, is a salve for the inner world that is quiet, needing stillness to be heard. When you do encounter it, the sound of silence is remarkable.

Take time in silence, whether meditating or simply walking in a forest. I spent five days in silence at a retreat center near my home. I arrived with some trepidation, as I had never done one before and wondered what I would do with all those hours on my own without technology or activity. It was a challenge. I brought some poetry, I took long walks in nature, I joined a group meditation every evening, I made a ritual of meals. On the final morning at breakfast, when another retreatant engaged me in conversation, it was jarring and unwelcome. I wasn't prepared to break the silence. It was a wonderfully deep bath in peace and calm that restored me and gave me the capacity to continue.

PATIENCE. One of the hallmarks of the feminine way of being with the darkness is to recognize the rhythms of time. Like giving birth, there is a patience required for gestation, waiting until the time is right rather than rushing. The birth will be when it will be. The seasons can't be hurried; they have their own rhythm and cadence. The same is true of the dark night. There is no way to hurry your way through it. It requires slowing down, waiting for the moment, releasing control. I spent months, perhaps years, trying to figure out how to speed things up and get back to normal as quickly as I could, with things just continuing to fall apart. Sheila did the same, ignoring the clues until she was finally dragged into the darkness.

Patience, though, is not the same as inactivity. There may be active work going on, but it is inner work, like completing the mourning of your losses before moving on, as Dirk and Charlotte are doing, or engaging in the ascent from the darkness slowly, as Mary is doing. Patience looks around, walks around, considers and ponders, before taking action.

SELF-COMPASSION. One of the easiest traps to fall into when you are feeling alienated from your current life but unsure where the pull is leading you is self-blame, belittling your feelings and urging yourself to just bloody well get on with it. You might reproach yourself for your moods and confusion, wondering what has happened and what is wrong with you.

It is a time for compassion, for being kind to yourself and allowing yourself to simply be with the fog. This can be difficult, especially for those of us who are driven by perfectionism. But it will ease your passage if you can have sympathy for your lot, as you might for a close friend or family member going through a hard time.

Into the Darkness

This stage is characterized by dissatisfaction, anxiety, questioning, foreboding, resistance, unraveling and breakdown. You might still be struggling to Band-Aid the status quo rather than recognizing the signs of a life structure ending. One of the challenges is not letting the breakdowns overwhelm you. Get help when you need it, rather than trying to manage on your own. The challenge is to engage with the darkness rather than turning away from it.

This might be a time to ask yourself how you are avoiding the changes you are being called to make. What aspects of your self-identity might you need to let go of? What values are most important to you at this time of your life? You might also ask yourself how you can simplify your lifestyle to make more quiet time, or challenge yourself to identify what you are afraid of.

Here are five coaching tips for entering the Into the Darkness stage of the dark night journey.

RECOGNIZE GATEKEEPERS. Gatekeepers are those well-meaning individuals who believe that you are better not to step over the threshold into the dark night passage. They are those who have a stake in you remaining who and where you are. They may have resisted their own calls from within and be afraid to lose you to that fearful territory. Will you still feel the same way about them? What if you don't return? These are important questions your loved ones may ask, consciously or not, and questions you may ask yourself as you consider opening that frightful door to the unknown.

Because the stakes are high, gatekeepers are highly skilled at finding reasons why it is not a good idea for you to answer the call to adventure. They will find appealing distractions to take you off the path and will take advantage of every "I told you so!" as you descend into the night. They may even resort to threatening dire consequences if you continue your folly.

For me, my husband was the gatekeeper. He simply wanted things to stay the same and watched helplessly as they fell apart, trying time and again to hold to our previously successful course. For Donald, it was his community at the ranch who didn't want change, who tried to protect him in their own ways. For Sheila, it was her fun-loving tribe of friends who didn't want her digging into her dark feelings and losing her light-heartedness.

Gatekeepers play an important role in proving the worth of our calling. If you are drawn forward despite their warnings, you know you must go in order to grow.

JOURNAL. I never considered myself good at journaling, but I bought a spiral notebook from time to time and began to do "morning pages" according to Julia Cameron's *The Artist's Way*. Three pages first thing every morning, just put the pen to the paper and write whatever comes to you. Much as I resisted, this practice helped me through a good deal of my early dark night experience, when I had little sense of what was happening or what to make of it. Then, in learning about Jungian practice, I was introduced to imaginative writing, a similar process of writing about a feeling, a memory, a dream, or a story you want to tell. This type of writing takes longer, ten to twenty minutes, and thus allows you to explore your topic more fully. You are encouraged to read what you have written aloud to yourself or someone else to hear the words as if someone else had written them.

I found this type of writing especially useful in the deep darkness, best when read aloud in a group as part of a shared process. And telling my story through writing this book has been a wonderful way to deepen my understanding of the nature of a dark night and my experience of it, much of it drawn from my journals.

You will find your own best journaling practice. There is no right or wrong way. You can ritually burn your journals or throw them out when you're on the other side. But there is great value in noting your progress, if only to yourself. It is a record of your experience, providing a track through the morass so you can see where you've been when you feel totally lost. When you feel like no one and nothing, it reminds you of the ground you've walked on.

BE CURIOUS. There is a question I came across, I'm not sure where. "What else is here?" I have asked myself this question many times when trying to discern another perspective, a paradox, or another side to the story. There is often no answer, but simply asking the question opens you to a broader viewpoint. Another I have come across is, "What do you mean by _____?" Fill in the blank. It's another way to dig deeper into the darkness. It is important to follow your intuition into whatever areas you are curious about. Ask the questions that trouble you and then seek out the answers, not as solutions but as perspectives on the issue, ways of seeing things differently, leaning into the opposite pole in your psyche.

Curiosity is meant to rupture your usual ways of thinking. This uprooting is important all the way through the dark night as you challenge your judgements, your assumptions and expectations, coming face to face with your shadows. You are not who you thought yourself to be, but who are you? The only way to know is to hold open the possibility, more strongly the probability, that you are misguided about everything you thought to be true.

Your curiosity may lead you to questions that grab you in the pit of your stomach and shake your foundations. These are authentic questions. Authentic questions often begin with "What" rather than "Why." "What" questions invite enquiry and narrative. They encourage a story. They are open-ended and inspire description or analysis. What is one important question you are curious about that you might ask yourself right now?

BE IN NATURE. Nature is one of your best allies through the darkness. As Rachel Carson wrote, "There is something infinitely healing in the repeated refrains of nature—the assurance that dawn comes after night, and spring after winter."[14] Nature is a wonderful salve and solace, a place where time is slowed, and birth and death co-exist in harmony.

When you are feeling lost and confused, nature provides a ground, a surety and a connection that can be a balm for the harried spirit. Charlotte, for example, spoke of finding solace only in cutting deadheads in her garden. Mary is finding beauty in her garden. The garden metaphor was very important in my dark night, too. There is something uniquely feminine about getting your hands into the soil, even if it's a few pots on your balcony or a window box full of herbs. Tending your garden, literally and metaphorically, is the creation of home. Commune with the trees, the ferns, the flowers—understand their rhythms, their acceptance, their timetable. Try touching the leaves as you pass or putting a gentle hand on the tree bark as you go by. Know that you are in a natural process that is connected to the cycle of life.

FEEL YOUR WAY THROUGH IT. This was a phrase I repeated to myself countless times through my dark night journey. Being someone who had relied on my thinking, I had to constantly remind myself that this was a feeling voyage and not only was my thinking *not* helpful but it was a serious detriment to my progress. Feeling my way through it put me in touch with my emotions, with my heart and my deeper intuitions, so I could act from a place of compassion and empathy for others and myself. This was particularly true for Sheila, too, who finally realized she had to take on her feelings rather than projecting them outward, to own them and work through them to become whole.

Disowning our feelings is quite natural. We have all been wounded by being rejected, hurt and disappointed. The feelings we experience break our tender hearts and we bury them in order to survive and thrive in a world we can't trust with our vulnerability. Dark nights are a reclaiming of our feelings, especially the ones we have disowned, from a place of greater maturity and acceptance, like Donald's learning to trust himself and his vulnerability and seeing it as a strength.

Navigating Your Underworld

Loss and Mourning

This stage is characterized by disorientation, fatigue, sadness, mourning, melancholy, depression, grief, and the sense of dying. You may feel stuck, absent, or preoccupied, or think your life has lost meaning. There are a couple of challenges at this stage. One is getting stuck in grief and depression. If you feel you can't carry on with your daily activities, get help. On the other extreme, you may try to move too quickly through the darkness, rather than taking the time to mourn your losses. You may even believe the darkness has gone when there is a temporary respite, and try to resume normal life rather than staying with the process. You will also have to find ways to leverage your limited energy.

At this time, you may want to ask yourself about the shadows you are uncovering that need atonement, or inquire into what you might do to bring a sense of joy into your day. You might ask yourself how to feel your losses deeply and what these losses have to teach you about yourself. Is there someone who you might connect with who has gone through a similar time?

Here are five coaching tips for moving through Loss and Mourning.

EAT AND SLEEP WELL, EXERCISE. This is the physical aspect of stepping into the dark night. You are using tremendous psychic energy. You are processing your thinking and feelings day and night. The darkness is a constant, demanding presence. Having the energy to experience the journey requires you to be your best, healthiest self, including your physical wellbeing. You may need more sleep, greater attention to diet and more regular exercise. I found I needed more sleep than usual. I was exhausted at the end of a day where I felt I hadn't done much of anything.

Mourning your losses may be especially difficult when your energy is used up in grief—when you feel depleted and depressed there is a tendency to ignore bodily needs, only exacerbating the problem of too little energy. I found as a diabetic that my blood glucose control was adversely affected for periods of time and I had to be particularly careful about what foods I ate unthinkingly as a way of stuffing my sorrow.

Exercise was a counterpoint to these difficulties. I loved walking, running, yoga, and skiing. Find an exercise you enjoy and make it a regular part of your routine, no matter how you are feeling in the moment. The endorphins it releases will reduce stress and increase positive moods. Illness and accidents are your body's way of getting your attention if you ignore your physical needs. Donald's bladder cancer and surgery earlier in his dark night journey was a wake-up call for him, similar to my broken bones and Nadine's car accidents.

HONOUR YOUR LOSSES. Losses are a large part of the dark night. You may, like me, lose friends and family, or a job and security, or a home and a sense of safety. You may lose physical wellbeing for a time. You may lose your spiritual path and feel that life is purposeless. You will almost certainly lose 'you' as you used to be. As in all of the stories here told, the losses may mount on top of each other, becoming a burden almost too heavy to bear. Charlotte describes this state of being in her story. "I am filled with such sadness and with tears that never seem to end."

It is critical to take the time to honour these losses. In our Western culture, there is a strong pull to move onward and upward, to get over our grief quickly, or at least to mourn on our own time. But that is precisely what grief takes—time. It can't be hurried or denied just because we don't talk about it. The process of mourning has its own imperatives. It is a process of sharing our thoughts and feelings with others in order to heal and become a reconciled person, not necessarily getting over the losses but being with them in a softer acceptance. Loss is a major part of every life. As we age, losses intensify for us and those around us. Being able to be with grief, to mourn and endure, is a signature strength in the dark night passage.

GET THERAPY. Talking it through with a professional could be a lifesaver when you are feeling stuck or puzzled and need to speak with someone who has no stake in your journey other than your wellbeing. A good counselor won't give you advice about how to be or what to do but will listen intently and feed your words back to you in a way that lets you hear yourself and perhaps reframe your feelings in a more helpful way. A coach can also be a guide who travels with you for a while and helps you unearth your internal hiding spots and explore their meaning. This was certainly the case for Sheila, who found coaching invaluable.

Therapy or coaching will not help if it is goal-directed or focused on problem-solving. A dark night is not a problem to be solved but an experience to be engaged in. If your therapist can support you being in the dark and work with you at whatever stage you are in to enrich your experience, then the role can be very helpful. There are coaches and therapists who specialize in deep transitions. Find one who speaks your language and inspires your confidence.

INCLUDE RITUALS. Robert Johnson, in *Owning Your Own Shadow,* says, "Remember, a symbolic or ceremonial experience is real and affects one as much as an actual event."[15] Rituals can help us mark the stages of our journey and ground us in celebrating successes, however small or tentative. I found dancing twice a week an important ritual. It was a way of letting go of everything and being in the moment, in the music, in interaction with others. I also structured my days ritualistically, eating the same foods at every breakfast and lunch, exercising, journaling, meditating, reading at the same times every day. These habits gave a certain grounding to my confusion. At least I could have some control over these basics!

I also created and participated in larger rituals: the full moon, the solstices, various festivals and celebrations. I attended a Unitarian church for a while. For Sheila and Dirk, astrology was a helpful grounding in a larger scheme of things. For Nadine, a channeler saw some signs worth watching for. For Donald, snowboarding is a spiritual ritual.

Anything that connects for you in a structured way can be a ritual that lights your path in the dark wood.

Rituals can be anything meaningful to you, from the sacred to the silly and everything in between. For example, a friend created a beautiful silver ring with six petals to honour six friends she has lost over the past couple of years. She calls it a gratitude ring. She uses the six petals not only to remember her friends but also in other ways, such as naming six things she's grateful for that day, or having six ideas about something she's trying to figure out. Having to come up with six items pushes her beyond the obvious.

SURRENDER. There are times during the long night when you may feel like you have hit a wall—there is nowhere to go and no hope in sight. Feelings of sadness and confusion can be paralyzing and can look like depression, that dark and painful place that takes over the deepest part of your being for a time. Marion Woodman writes about this suffering, "a sense of loss of all, even the capacity for action, a loss so deep nothing matters, pitched past pitch of grief."[16] Dark nights are initiations, death and rebirth processes, rites of passage. As such, they require a surrender of some of your most closely held beliefs. It is necessarily a time of suffering, of letting go.

You may need to hit the wall. Many of us do because we hold on so tightly to our conditioning. I held on for several years, as did both Sheila and Nadine. But if you can see it coming, if you understand the transition process, if you know that surrendering to the cycle of renewal is the way to steer clear of the wall, then perhaps you can veer in time to avoid spending what feels like ages in the deep dark. The surrender of your egoic self usually happens all along the way and at some level you know you will survive.

Meeting the Discarded Other

This stage is characterized by feeling dead, naked, withdrawn, empty, and still. You may experience nothingness, lethargy, torpor. You may also begin to experience revelation, insight, germination, trust, and forgiveness. One of the challenges at this stage is sitting with your small self, with your unacknowledged shadows, rather than becoming distracted. You may find it challenging to atone for the transgressions you have unearthed, forgiving yourself and others. Or you may find it difficult to identify and reclaim the Discarded Other you have abandoned, and to see how this Other came to be.

This is a good time to ask yourself how you might see what has happened as a spiritual path. What are the patterns, the repeating images or polarities, the paradoxes that characterize your journey so far? And what hopeful signs can you identify?

Here are five coaching tips to guide you through Meeting the Discarded Other.

DISCOVER THE POLARITY. The dark night passage is a quest in search of an Other, a polar opposite to who we think we are, an element of ourselves we have discarded in order to maintain our self-concept, our ego. The psyche's polarities will call out when an imbalance becomes too great, when we are essentially lying to ourselves about who we truly are. The call from the Underworld is the Discarded Other crying out for recognition and reconciliation. The acknowledgement of this Other existing outside our consciousness, and our reconciliation with it, is the route to wholeness.

However, to do so requires a figurative death and rebirth, surrendering our former self and allowing our new identity to emerge, bringing both poles into consciousness.

The Other in your story may not be obvious for some time. It can be buried under layers of self-protection that make it difficult to pinpoint until you are well into the journey. Whatever specific shape your path takes, it will unite the symbolic psychic poles of inner and outer, masculine and feminine. Reflect on what pulls and scratches at the corners of your mind. It may be where you find your buried treasure.

LISTEN IN STILLNESS. Listening deeply is one of the most underrated capacities in adults today and it is at the core of the dark night journey. Of course, listening to guides, mentors, coaches, therapists, friends and loved ones is important, discerning from their perspectives what is relevant to your current issues. But perhaps even more important is listening to yourself, listening deeply to what is happening within. You are trained to listen for information from your environment—not only what is said but what is not said, in body language, expression, and other clues. You take in and process enormous amounts of information every minute of every day. However, you likely have received precious little training in inner listening, tuning in to your internal environment, your psyche and the clues you are sending yourself from your deeper wells.

It is to these undercurrents you must listen in the darkness. This listening requires solitude, contemplation, surrendering your assumptions and opening to allow more of your deepest self to emerge and tell you what it wants you to hear. Eventually, you will listen for a shift in your identity. Donald recognized such a shift when he said, "I now allow things to be rather than to think I need to change so much of

196

what happens in life." Or as Nadine says, "I don't need to be creating some big idea, just small, simple and personal is OK, just my own intention and attention." Listening for these deeper insights requires a level of stillness that is difficult to sustain. But when you listen from this open field, you often hear surprising messages that may shape your future.

ATTEND TO INEFFABLES. Ineffables are those things you can't describe or explain by ordinary means. They are synchronicities, symbols, phrases, or clues that have special meaning and connection for you at certain times in your journey. They usually arrive with a wash of warm feeling that is a kind of knowing. It's not an intellectual knowing but is more fundamental than that, deep in the body, accompanied by a sense of peace. Ineffables are the perfect integration of thinking and feeling. They are what make a dark night a spiritual journey. There is nothing in your factual experience to account for them. And yet they happen frequently, if you're open and curious.

I had many of these ineffable moments, and although I was skeptical at first, I came to trust them as time went on. They came from many sources: meditation, reading, poetry, conversation, shamanic experiences, and my own writing. They were often a short phrase or metaphor I had to ponder and could see from different angles, what the Zen Buddhists call a Koan, a riddle. "There is more." "I have inherited a garden." "I am that I AM." Nadine tells of her download, "Fire yourself!" Your particular ineffables will come according to your circumstances and needs.

FIND MEANING IN MYTH. During the dark night, myths provide another way of connecting to the enduring nature of these transformative processes and their common characteristics, allowing you to see yourself as part of a larger, timeless human story.

Myths are often immortalized through gods and goddesses whose stories reflect these characteristics. The myth of the goddess Inanna and her dark sister Ereshkigal highlighted the circular dark night process for me, introducing me to the nature of the dark feminine hidden in the underworld longing for reunion with the light. Their story is included in the Appendix. Hestia was also helpful in connecting me to home and hearth and its importance in my life.

WATCH FOR DISTRACTIONS. One of the most common salves for our confusion is to turn toward the many outward distractions that come to us during the dark night. They are so very appealing! They are the ordinary (or sometimes extraordinary) opportunities that seem to be dropped, like manna from heaven, in front of us to tempt us from our path.

For me, my repeated renovations were a distraction, searching for home in all the wrong places. Nadine was similar in moving back and forth from Canada to New Zealand, searching for belonging and coming up empty.

It is helpful to slow your decision making about taking on new projects, avoiding those knee-jerk decisions that can become all-consuming and rob your energy from your real purpose. As Charlotte comments, "the default is always there when you come back . . . you come home and there is this loss of energy."

What might your ego distractions be? They aren't always grand opportunities or upheavals but just psychic numbing through things like television, surfing the Internet, playing computer games, or losing yourself in alcohol or drugs. These might all be necessary at certain points to take a break from the intensity of your inner turmoil but if they are more than that, they will simply leave you dissatisfied.

Navigating Your Ascent

Rebirth and its Sacrifices

At this stage you may feel an awakening, excitement mixed with sadness, renewed energy. You may feel fresh, fragile, vulnerable, emotional, tentative, compassionate and humble. One of the challenges in building a new identity is taking it slowly, feeling your way into your new world and noticing the changes since you've been away. You may also find it difficult to acknowledge the sacrifices that have been necessary—to feel the remorse, guilt and regret.

This may be a time to ask yourself how you can protect your fragile wings as you begin to fly. What do you need to hold on to and what do you need to let go of in this new chapter? Who are the three most important people you need to connect with now? Or you might ponder on the temptations that might entice you to move too swiftly through this stage.

Here are four coaching tips to help guide you through the stage of Rebirth and Its Sacrifices.

<u>**EXPECT SETBACKS AND SURPRISES.**</u> Although I've described and demonstrated a process through the dark night with somewhat predictable stages, it is important to remember that this is not a linear process. It's more like wheels within wheels, circles extending beyond circles in a process of fits and starts, leaps and bounds, then halts and pauses. It is possible, even probable, that you will be stuck in one stage or another for periods of time.

Mary resisted the call from her underworld for several years. Charlotte is stuck in mourning, feeling there is an unending series of losses she must endure. Dirk is waiting in the darkness for some clarity of purpose with his new limitations. You may come to a halt, as I did, at the stage of surrendering your current life and ways of being, feeling like you're in a life-and-death struggle. Nadine describes the repetitive cycles of accidents and incidents until she finally could not go on as before and had to stop.

There is even a tendency to get stuck in the ascent, either rising too quickly, only to be thrown back into the darkness, or finding the relief from suffering so appealing that there is no momentum left for moving into the Integration phase and your new life. There may be a waiting period needed to gather your strength for re-entry. Be open, expect delays, messes, setbacks and surprises along the way, and welcome them as strangers to get to know. One of the lessons of the darkness is its uncertainty. When you think you have the answer, there will be something unexpected to assure you that you do not.

BE CREATIVE. The arts in all their forms are wonderful outlets all along the path but especially as you begin again. Painting, drawing, collaging, writing, poetry, movies, theatre, music—do whatever appeals to you, whether you create it yourself or participate in what others have produced.

A friend and I had several painting weekends. We would go to the galleries and look at the art to feel inspired, then come back and paint together, creating something motivated by what we had seen. We would then celebrate our accomplishment with dinner and a toast to our creativity. These brief outings were like spaces out of time, when I could enter another dimension of reality and express it on canvas.

For Mary, her garden expresses her creative self. For Nadine, planting trees puts her in touch with her homeland. For Donald, his horses anchor and connect him to his trusting self. Find your creative avenues and explore them, either individually or with others. In becoming whole, balancing the analytical and creative is critical.

RECONNECT. There will come a time when you recognize a new spaciousness, sense of joy, gratitude, and abundance. Like a butterfly emerging from the cocoon, you tentatively test your wings to see if you can fly. You are beautiful! You will begin to reconnect with the world around you, slowly shaping a new identity out of the ashes of the old. It is a time for experimenting, exploring, evaluating, discerning what becomes you and what does not. You may want to reconnect with people, places, activities, and interests that have been set aside or that are now newly appealing.

The danger is in making decisions too quickly, before you have created your whole new Self. Take your time. Give yourself permission to test the water, to be shy about getting to know your new individuality. You will also want to give yourself permission to avoid situations that don't encourage your new identity to flourish—avoiding family drama, or spending time with certain friends.

LET GO. There is a final reckoning as you emerge from the darkness, a price to be paid for the gift of new awareness. Like the albatross, always there at the edge of your view, this torment may have been following you for some time, but you have hoped for some way out. And although the change may manifest in the external world, it is the newly integrated psyche that is seeing everything in a new light, with new eyes, and looking for you to restore that balance in your life. For me, my marriage was the ultimate sacrifice I had to make to begin again on my own terms. For Donald, the sacrifice was the loss of his brother and closest friends. For Nadine, it was the sacrifice of her dream of building an intentional community.

This kind of letting go involves deep psychic change and can cloud the joy of rebirth. Survival has a cost. However, it does not necessarily mean you have to end your dreams or relationships. It may be that you can die to those that don't fit as they were and rebirth them as they can now be, using your new awareness and connection to recreate them, stronger and deeper than before. As you experiment, you will know what needs to be shed and what can be transformed.

Restoration and Integration

This final stage is characterized by clarity, relief, gratitude, wholeness, grace, surprise, openness, connection, expansiveness, play, positivity, energy and enthusiasm. It may be challenging to believe you're actually in a whole new world; you may expect to fall back into the darkness again. Another challenge might be expecting everything about the future to be perfect and full of light, now that you've survived the journey. It can also feel awkward at first to find your way.

This is a time to ask yourself what you have learned from your experience. Who are you now? As you reflect on your journey, what are the themes that have emerged most strongly for you? You might also ask how you will take the gifts from your dark night passage into the world. What might your contribution to the whole be?

Here are three coaching tips for moving through the Restoration and Integration stage.

PLAY AND CELEBRATE. Finally, it is time to celebrate having achieved the passage into wholeness. Congratulations! Let yourself really feel the energy and excitement and find ways to express it in the world. Many adults have either never known or have forgotten how to play. Find a kindred spirit or two and create some play dates together. It can be as simple as a walk in the park or a visit to a museum or gallery. It can be playing cards or games with friends— anything that brings joy and a chance to laugh out loud. You may also want to look at your calendar and purge it of activities that don't bring you joy.

Your loved ones may be delighted to join with you in this celebrating. They will have been through their own version of the dark night as they watched you struggle and will need to see and hear from you that you are back from your journey, a different you for them to get to know over time. You may have difficulty describing the changes at first, but they will show up in your attitudes and behaviour as they reveal themselves. You might spend an evening with close friends to celebrate your rebirth. Or cook dinner for your partner or significant other and tell them how you're feeling. You might make a list of new ways you want to show up in the world.

TELL YOUR STORY. One of the contributions you can make is to tell your story. This is not only a cathartic experience, it is also one of the best ways to weave the important aspects of your particular passage into a tapestry that represents the wholeness you feel. And since you are one of many people who will go through this dark night, your contribution to our understanding of the territory is vital in supporting others. In the Contributors section at the end of this book, the storytellers have offered their insights into having their perspectives articulated through their telling and my writing of their journeys.

You can use any of the prompts in this book as a way to get started: the process map, the stages, the stories, the themes. You can write your story, record it, draw or paint it, sculpt it, dance it, or create a play. Choose whatever medium you feel reflects the core of what you want to convey so that your means of expression adds to the depth of your telling.

SHARE YOUR GIFTS. The gifts you receive from your dark night passage are meant to be shared. You are now responsible for taking the insights, ideas, experiences and understanding you have gained into your family, your work and life, your community, and the world. You could create a storyboard of your intentions, using magazine pictures and words glued onto cardstock, and placing it so you can refer to it often. You need not achieve great things; in fact, quite the opposite. Be your whole self in the most ordinary ways, every day. Your role is to embrace and embody your new consciousness as a model for others, in gratitude and humility.

Your contributions beyond that will come to you in their time. Each of us who has made the journey is in a unique position to influence the dark night of the world, to see the larger picture. It is to this work that we can now turn, each with our own ways and means. For Donald, it is contributing to new regulations to combat the water crisis in his valley. For Sheila, it is sponsoring dialogues to generate alternatives for dealing with wicked problems like climate change. For me, it has to do with creating conversations about dying.

You will find your own ways of navigating your dark night. As long as you attend to your inner experience and find ways to communicate and express it, you will find with time that you awaken into a new kind of grace.

Summary of Part Three Offerings

The Twelve Themes

INWARD-TURNING

QUESTIONING

DISCONTINUITY

SHADOW WORK

TRANSFORMATION

DREAMS

ATTACHMENTS

SUPPORT

IMAGES AND METAPHORS

METAPHORS

DEATH

MYSTICAL MYSTERIES

The Coaching Perspectives

The Descent
The Call from the Psyche

ACCEPTANCE
MINDFULNESS
SILENCE
PATIENCE
SELF-COMPASSION

Into the Darkness

RECOGNIZE GATEKEEPERS
JOURNAL
BE CURIOUS
BE IN NATURE
FEEL YOUR WAY THROUGH IT

The Underworld
Loss and Mourning

EAT & SLEEP WELL, EXERCISE
HONOUR YOUR LOSSES
GET THERAPY
RITUALS
SURRENDER

Meeting the Discarded Other

DISCOVER THE POLARITY
LISTEN IN STILLNESS
ATTEND TO INEFFABLES
FIND MEANING IN MYTH
WATCH FOR DISTRACTIONS

The Ascent
Rebirth & Its Sacrifices

EXPECT SETBACKS
BE CREATIVE
RECONNECT
LET GO

Restoration & Integration

PLAY & CELEBRATE
TELL YOUR STORY
SHARE YOUR GIFTS

[14] Carson, Rachel. "The Real World Around Us," in *Lost Woods: The discovered writing of Rachel Carson* (Boston: Beacon Press, 1999), 23.

[15] Johnson, Robert A. *Owning Your Own Shadow: Understanding the dark side of the psyche* (New York: HarperCollins, 1991), 52.

[16] Woodman, *Conscious Femininity*, 36.

Conclusion

It's already turned loose. It's already coming.
It can't be called back.
. . . Karen Marmon Silko

In the end, what we are letting go of in the dark night is our illusions. The way we have held reality shifts and we see the world differently. We see that what we have taken to be real is actually not—it is just a way of looking, and we can now see from a broader perspective.

The dark night is a letting go of the illusion of *me* as the center of existence. The ego is simply the mind working to keep a lid on things, to structure experience into categories so we won't be afraid or uncertain, a need to control through ideas, frameworks, concepts, contexts. When we are reborn after a dark night, a death of the too-powerful ego, there may be a shock of understanding and a bewilderment about our new circumstances. It is literally a *whole* new world!

What we sacrifice is our illusion of being in control, of being able to figure it out using only our logical ways of knowing. Instead we are given the gift of new sight, of seeing more of what we are: a dynamic unity of opposites in every dimension, a wave and particle complementarity in a constant energetic flux and flow, the psychic polarities in a relational dance. We are more whole in the sense that we see more clearly the whole of this reality and our place in it.

Part of the new sense of place is also letting go of *me* as separate from *us* and *all of us,* whether all of us as people—past, present and future—or all of nature, from the smallest molecule to the vast cosmos. We are the others we have discarded in all of the polarities, and with a gentle inhale we bring them together throughout time and space. We really are One.

Dark night passages are iterative. What we see anew now is also illusory. As these ways of seeing become more familiar, we move through their patterns and deceptions until perhaps we again make a leap into another tier of consciousness, another letting go of illusions, through another dark night. And so it goes until in death we return to our essence, our soul, our story told, adding to the chronicle of tales told by our ancestors of their lives, and of their leadership in facing the darkness of their generations.

In that vein, I end as I began with a story. It is offered not as prediction but as preparation—let us act while we have time.

I am sitting in a powerful wisdom circle at a weekend workshop held in the beautiful celebration hall of a cemetery here in Vancouver. We are gathered around a huge copper bowl full of small white stones and candles of various sizes, our metaphoric fire, encircled with the symbolic objects we have each brought with us to witness our work over the next couple of days. We are here to dig into the themes I have recently been playing with, dark night gifts I have been given, to see where they may take us. Two dear friends and I have assembled this group to weave a web of care and concern for the planet, for our communities, for ourselves, and for our future possibilities. Our invitation lists these three recognitions:

- The Dark Night—of the self, the community, the world
- The Fire—at our door, in our belly, bringing major change
- The Feminine—the dark feminine arising and convening.

These recognitions have emerged more clearly for me over the past year. Firstly, I have realized that the dark night is endemic in our culture at every level. For example, as I have talked about writing this book, I have found people connecting with the truth of their own dark nights, acknowledging that they are in one, or have been, or even that they wished they were, to move them out of their doldrums. When I look at our communities, I see they are often places of isolation and injustice rather than peace and connection. And we are all too aware of the planetary crises of our times, the dark night of our world whether social,

213

environmental, political, psychological, or economic. This notion of a dark night seems to be ever more present, clear and distressing at both individual and collective levels.

The second recognition came at my annual shamanic retreat this year. I received a very strong message that "a fire is coming," a fire that will blow through everything and change the world as we know it. I have spent a lot of time wondering about this mysterious download. What am I to do with the information? It could be a year, a decade, or a millennium, although given our current conditions I doubt it will be that long. Does it mean a planetary disaster, an environmental collapse? A nuclear winter? The end of humanity? Or possibly it is simply a recognition that things are going to get a lot worse before they get better.

Perhaps it is also a metaphor for inner change, a fire in our bellies. Fire is a metaphor for our inner divine spark, the psychic flame that longs for harmony. If left untended, this spark can become a raging fire, a bonfire of our vanities, the psyche at war with itself to a metaphorical death and rebirth. This is Kali, the dark goddess whose rage uproots and destroys. This is also Mother Earth, who is already unleashing her wrath at our negligence.

By whatever means this burning of old ways unfolds, I am more and more struck by the feminine rising, the third recognition, something like the phoenix from the ashes, to demand restitution. It could be that this is the discarded feminine (yin) consciousness erupting in rage and grief, demanding an integrated relationship with the dominant masculine (yang) psychic energy. The dark night and the dark feminine have much in common: healing through transformation, destruction before reconstruction, the unconscious becoming conscious, all in the name of producing a new wholeness. Is this dark feminine energy the fire that is coming? Maybe we are meant to rise up out of our discarded depths to burn away the layers of our own and our culture's illusions. Will we erupt in fiery fury? Or fiery love? This could be the moment of death before new life, a season of darkness and decay that germinates renewal. I wonder if we have the necessary fire in our bellies to finally wake us up to the call of alienation and suffering within and without. I don't have answers. What I feel is the fire coming, the feminine rising and the call to restore equilibrium through a dark night that we must answer.

This has been my own story, the fire that has blown through my life changing everything over the past half dozen years, my own feminine rising out of the ashes of my dark night, but as I sit in the circle on this weekend hearing from others, I realize I am not alone. We are hungry for change, for contribution to a different future. As we listen to each other's stories, we are empowered to weave new insights, ideas and actions for moving forward. We begin by admitting the darkness and welcoming its gifts into the space. We acknowledge that a fire is coming, in fact perhaps already here, bringing an end to many of our current ways of being. And we appreciate that the feminine rising is not a takeover, it's a merger with the masculine to create greater wholeness. The feminine rising through the fire of the dark night is a realignment required in each of us to bring ourselves and our societies into harmony.

With these three recognitions in mind—the dark night, the fire coming, the feminine rising—we return to the central questions. What do we see in the world? What is our role in influencing this societal dark night journey? We see the signs of breakdown within us and around us. And yet we resist, though we know a transformation of our way of life is required, a radical shift in our fundamental worldview.

We huddle together and let the darkness descend. We invite each other to turn inward and answer the call to a different kind of adventure, one we have perhaps been loath to undertake. For this dark night journey is a renewal, a rebirth to a new way of being—spacious, selfless, generative—that is sorely needed by the world right now. If we are successful, what evolves from these collective dark nights will not be so much a role or an organization but more a social movement, thousands of different skillful means of contributing, where we know we are part of something larger than ourselves, we connect with confidence and play our parts. We mention the feminist movement (Me Too), the environmental movement (climate change), and the civil rights movement (Black Lives Matter). We begin to shape how we can be involved, each in our unique ways, to change the status quo. What kind of leadership can we provide; what wisdom and experience can we offer?

We end our weekend circle with a common commitment. Let those of us in the *me* generation become a *we* generation as we emerge from our dark night passages. We have the freedom and responsibility to discover the next evolutionary unfolding of what it means to be wholly human, laying down new tracks into the future, packing with us the strengths of our experience and adding to it an expansive new awareness as seasoned sages leading from our whole selves on behalf of the whole world.

But before we can take up this call to share our gifts, we must prepare by undertaking a developmental journey. We must wake up those areas of our personality that wait in darkness, hidden away from consciousness: our denials, addictions and withholdings. It is here that the seeds of our unique leadership contribution lie, buried deep in the earth awaiting the light of awareness.

Let this be an invitation, an invocation and a call to action, a radical manifesto for living and leading in the next thirty years. We can tend the fire before it gets out of control, bank the flames so the death and rebirth process can proceed. Let us wake up—we have our *whole* lives ahead of us!

Appendix
The Dark Feminine in Myth

A myth is essentially a culture's fundamental worldview in narrative form, defining and explaining the values and ideals of the day, originally told in dramatic fashion through the activities of gods and goddesses. In early Greek times, these figures were often named for natural elements, such as Poseidon for water, Apollo for sun, and Aphrodite for desire, embodying powerful forces beyond human control. Myths were expressed in speeches, poetry and plays, told repeatedly in the oral tradition and adapted to the needs of the times, gradually becoming part of literature and lore. They were less practically factual than they were a means to shape social behaviour and religious thought. Today, myths are understood to be part of every culture, referring to the underlying patterns of a society's goals, fears, ambitions and dreams. Mythological themes are often used as frameworks for modern storytelling and expressed through a variety of media to audiences all over the world.

Joseph Campbell has been referred to as the father of modern mythological studies, comparing myths through time to create a "monomyth," a universal structure for storytelling that has been used across time and geography, what he calls "the hero's journey." His story structure has been used countless times in movies, including *Indiana Jones, The Matrix* and *The Lion King.* In *The Hero with a Thousand Faces,* Campbell explains that as humans we need some way of describing the unfathomable and the ineffable, and we do that through the use of metaphors found in myths. These metaphors allow us to describe the transcendent beyond everyday words—the psychic unity of darkness and light, conscious and unconscious that bring us into wholeness.

Inasmuch as Campbell's monomyth reflects underlying social patterns through time, it also reflects a masculine bias toward the hero, the male adventurer who is supported by female nurturers, guides and challengers on the road to replacing the patriarchal father as head of the kingdom. So although included in his interpretations, the feminine, and particularly the dark feminine, is underplayed and deserves highlighting for its distinctive perspective in myths through the ages.

The dark feminine is represented by what I have called the Discarded Other, that core part of our psyche we have repressed. She is the dark sister held in the shadows of the unconscious. Our attachment to the monomyth and our resistance to its feminine counterpart leave our current culture dangerously out of balance. If we do not turn inward to recognize this essential hidden quality in ourselves and expose it to the light, its powerful dark energy can erupt into consciousness, bringing with it rage, fear, greed, prejudice or addiction.

Many of the feminine goddesses embody this dark energy and its potential for fiery eruption. For example, Kali, the black Hindu goddess of death and violence, stands with her multiple arms arrayed for battle on the body of her husband, the lord Shiva. As with many of the feminine myths, she has a light counterpart sister, Parvati, who is said to have shed her dark skin to create Kali, the fierce Other.

Sekhmet is another powerful warrior goddess, portrayed in Egyptian mythology as a lioness with a red sun, the colour of blood, on her head. Her role is to protect justice and balance in all things. She represents a fiery power and harsh strength that can be destructive. Her sister counterpart is Hathor, a gentle, friendly sister who is full of joy, laughter and dance.

In the Christian tradition there is the Black Madonna, the dark feminine counterpart to the Virgin Mary. Statues of the ancient Black Madonna have been discovered throughout Europe, representing the dark pole of the feminine, the unconscious, mysterious and unpredictable. She is said to have descended from Isis, the Eqyptian goddess, as both divine and nocturnal. However, only the pure light of the Virgin was incorporated into the sacred texts, discarding the threatening dark sister.

There are numerous other powerful, dark feminine goddesses worth exploring: Lilith in early Jewish mythology, Medusa in somewhat later Greek mythology, or Pele of Hawaiian mythology. One of my favourites is the Greek goddess Hestia, or Vesta to the Romans, who was fire itself, representing the warmth of hearth and home rather than a fiery destroyer. She symbolized the embracing spirit I longed for in my search for a home where I belonged.

The twinning or sisterhood repeated in these different mythologies suggests the importance of the relationship between the poles of the psyche, the unconscious and conscious, the masculine and feminine, as they dynamically interact. One of the oldest and best-known feminine myths is the story of Innana and her dark sister Ereshkigal.[17] I tell a version of it here to give a sense of how a myth can portray this integration and can be an allegory for life and death, the seasons, the sun and moon, and other mutual relationships.

The Myth of Inanna

Six thousand years ago in ancient Sumeria, Inanna is worshipped as the Goddess of Love and War. She is all-powerful, free to roam the vast regions of heaven and earth, and when she receives the gift of the divine laws of the universe, she becomes a radiant ruler of her people.

One day, Inanna suddenly hears the sound of her sister's moans. Ereshkigal, Inanna's sister, is Queen of the Underworld, and it seems impossible that her cries could reach to the heavens, but it is true. Inanna hears her long and terrible wails, for Ereshkigal has suffered loss and is in pain.

"I must go to my dark sister in hell," she tells her servant, Ninshubur.

"You must not go," Ninshubur cries. "No one returns from the Underworld."

But Inanna is determined to see her sister, to understand The Great Below by experiencing death, and so she instructs her servant, "If I do not return in three days, you must go to seek help from the gods. They will rescue me."

Then Inanna prepares for the descent. Dressed in flowing royal robes, she places a crown of blazing gold upon her head. Around her neck she wears beads of lapis lazuli. She wears bracelets on her wrists and rings on her fingers. She wears a breastplate adorned with jewels, and she takes along a measuring rod and line. She is prepared to leave everything else she has ever known behind. Ninshubur is certain she will never see her mistress again.

When Inanna arrives at the outer gates of the Underworld, she challenges the gatekeeper, Neti, to allow her to pass. "I must consult with Ereshkigal," Neti says. He hurries to Inanna's sister to describe the great and powerful goddess dressed in jewels who awaits entrance at the gate of the Underworld. Ereshkigal envies and despises her powerful and carefree sister, and so she instructs her gatekeeper, "Open the seven gates," she says, "but only the smallest crack. As my sister enters each gate, take another of her royal garments from her."

And so Neti opens the first gate. Inanna, about to pass through, gasps as the gatekeeper removes her dazzling crown. "Why?" Inanna asks.

"Quiet, Inanna. The ways of the Underworld are different. I cannot answer your questions," Neti replies. At the second gate, Neti takes away Inanna's beads, and again the goddess asks him, "Why?"

"Our ways are not your ways," Neti answers. At the third gate he removes her breastplate of sparkling stones. At the fourth gate, he takes away her bracelets, and at the fifth he snatches her rings. Inanna gasps again when Neti takes her measuring rod while she slips through the sixth gate, and when she finally reaches the last gate, she barely resists as he removes her beautiful royal robe and ushers her naked through the seventh gate.

224

Now defenseless, Inanna enters bowed low. She walks into her sister's throne room and looks up at her dark sister. She sees the eye of death staring back at her. "Sister," Ereshkigal says, but that is all she says before she strikes Inanna dead. Inanna is hung from a peg and left to rot.

Meanwhile Ninshubur waits, and when three days have passed with no sign of her mistress, she flees to seek Enlil's help, for he is God of the Air. "I cannot help," he tells the weeping servant. "The Underworld is not my domain. Your mistress should not have ventured so far." Ninshubur runs to Nanna, Goddess of the Moon, but Nanna shakes her head. "I have no rule over the Underworld," she says. And so at last Ninshubur visits Enki, God of Wisdom and Water, and Inanna's grandfather. It is he, after all, who originally blessed Inanna with the gift of the universal laws, for he knew that without Inanna, life on earth would die. From beneath his fingernails, Enki takes dirt and with this he creates two new creatures. "Go to the Underworld and give these gifts to Inanna," he instructs the creatures as he hands them goblets filled with the food and water of life.

Able to adopt any disguise, the creatures turn themselves into flies and slip unnoticed through the cracks at each of the seven gates of the Underworld. When they reach the throne room, they hear Ereshkigal's moans. "Oh, my heart and soul," she weeps and the creatures echo

Ereshkigal's words back to her. "Oh, my heart and soul," they moan with her. They moan with compassion and understanding, and compassion is what Ereshkigal craves most. At last she grows silent and, turning to those who seem to feel empathy for her pain, she offers them any gift they desire. "Give us Inanna's body," the creatures ask.

Ereshkigal gives them Inanna's body, and they feed the goddess the food and water of life. And so Inanna ascends, knowing that what she has learned about herself and about life demands sacrifice, and so before she can return to heaven and earth for good, according to the universal laws, a substitute, one of her dearest loved ones, must be found to take her place and live in the dark Underworld.

Inanna returns to earth in search of someone to substitute for her. All the way to the palace, her people weep and mourn her absence and the earth has begun to decay. All except her husband Dumuzi, who sits on her throne dressed as a king and playing the flute. When Inanna sees this, she chooses Dumuzi to live in the Underworld as his punishment, but his compassionate sister volunteers to serve his sentence for six months of every year. Inanna is moved by this gesture of true love and compassion, and so brother and sister serve equally. In this way, the cycle of life begins again each spring when Dumuzi returns to join

Inanna, the king and queen wedded to the earth. Inanna has united in herself the upper and lower worlds. Her power and wisdom are greater than ever. She is magnificent.

The myth of Innana has many parallels to the stories in this book. She has lived in the upper world, in the light and in her masculine power. She hears the call from her dark feminine sister who is held in darkness, in the Underworld. She has ignored her own darkness and is called to confront it. She prepares with all her material worldly possessions, believing they will help her, but they are no good to her in her inner work and world. She must leave them all behind and surrender to different powers.

To accomplish her journey in the Underworld, she must die to her former self and be united with her sister, her dark side. She must incorporate her own darkness, her denied feelings, her shadows. Ereshkigal is her Discarded Other. She is aided by her humble servant Ninshubur and her wise grandfather Enki, as well as the caring creatures he sends. It is the creatures' feeling qualities of empathy and compassion for Ereshkigal's pain that ultimately save Inanna, because Ereshkigal mourns her loss of connection, yearning for warmth and kindness. It is this call from the discarded feminine that Inanna hears and responds to.

When Inanna is restored, she must suffer some sacrifice to be reborn. She must send someone she loves, some part of her former self that she is attached to, into darkness so she never forgets this aspect of her consciousness. The passage between the light and dark must be maintained to be whole. And so Dumuzi must also descend as a male and undergo the same initiation as Inanna. He must "go to hell" so that he too may be made whole by finding his lost feminine. Here he is aided by his compassionate sister, his own inner feminine, who agrees to share his fate. By sharing each year, the cycles of sun and moon, harvest and fallow seasons, masculine and feminine, are sustained. The king and queen become true partners, wedded to each other, allowing the kingdom to flourish.

[17] Kleiner, Liliana. *The Song of Inanna*. A Hand Made Artist Book. www.lilianakleiner.com.

References

Akamolafe, Bayo. "Why Shadows were Invented." Accessed
March 21, 2019.
*http://www.dailygood.org/story/2243/why-
shadows-were-invented-bayo-akomolafe/.*

Alighieri, Dante. *Divine Comedy: Inferno, Pergatorio,
Paradiso.* London: Everyman's Library, 1995.

Berry, Wendell. *The Selected Poems of Wendell Berry.*
Berkeley: Counterpoint, 1999.

Bolen, Jean Shinoda. *Goddesses in Older Women:
Archetypes in women over fifty.* New York: Harper,
2014.

Brecht, Bertold. John Willett & Ralph Manheim Eds. *Poems
1913-1956.* North Yorkshire: Eyre Methuen, 1976.

Brown, Michael. *The Presence Process: A journey into
present moment awareness.* Vancouver: Namaste
Publishing, 2010.

Cameron, Julia. *The Artist's Way: A spiritual path to higher
creativity.* New York: Tarcher Perigree, 2016.

Campbell, Joseph. *The Hero with a Thousand Faces.*
Princtron NJ: Princeton University Press, 1973.

Carroll, Lewis. *Alice in Wonderland.* Ware UK: Wordsworth
Editions Ltd., 2018.

Carson, Rachel. "The Real World Around Us." In: *Lost Woods: The discovered writing of Rachel Carson*, edited by Linda Lear. Boston: Beacon Press, 1999, pages 199 - 209.

Chodron, Pema. *When Things Fall Apart: Heart advice for difficult times*. Boulder CO: Shambala, 2016.

Cohen, Leonard. *The Future*. Toronto: McClelland & Stewart, 1993.

Erickson, Milton and Ernest Lawrence Rossi. *The February Man: Evolving consciousness and identity in hypnotherapy*. New York: Routledge, 1989.

Estes, Clarissa Pinkola. *Women Who Run with the Wolves: Myths and stories of the wild woman archetype*. New York: Ballantine Books, 1997.

Fischer, Angela. "Entering the Secret." In *The Unknown She: Eight Faces of an emerging consciousness*, by Hilary Hart. Inverness CA: The Golden Sufi Center, 2004, pages 19 - 61.

Fitzgerald, F. Scott. *The Crack-Up: With other uncollected pieces, note-books and unpublished letters*. New York: New Directions, 1956.

Gebser, Jean. *The Ever-Present Origin: Foundations of the aperspectival world*. Athens OH: Ohio University Press, 1986.

Grof, Christina & Stanislav. *The Stormy Search for the Self.*
New York: Penguin, 1990.

Gustafson, Fred. *The Black Madonna of Einsiedeln: An
ancient image for our present time.* Einsiedeln:
Diamon Verlag, 2009.

Hamilton, Diane Musho. "Willing to Feel." Accessed March
21, 2019. https://tendirections.com/willing-to-feel/.

Harvey, Andrew. *The Sun at Midnight: A memoir of the dark
night.* New York: Tarcher, 2002.

Hillman, James. *The Soul's Code: In search of character and
calling.* New York: Grand Central Publishing, 1997.

Hirsch, Edward. *For the Sleepwalkers.* Pittsburgh PA:
Carnegie Mellon, 1998.

Hollis, James. *Living an Examined Life: Wisdom for the
second half of the journey.* Louisville CO: Sounds
True, 2018.

Jenkinson, Stephen. *Come of Age: The case for elderhood in
a time of trouble.* Berkeley CA: North Atlantic Books,
2018.

Johnson, Robert A. *Owning Your Own Shadow:
Understanding the dark side of the psyche.* Toronto:
Harper Collins, 1991.

Jung, C.G. *Man and his Symbols.* Toronto: Dell Publishing,
1968.

Kegan, Robert and Lahey, Lisa. *Immunity to Change: How to Overcome It and Unlock the Potential in Yourself and Your Organization*. Boston MA: Harvard Press, 2009.

Kingsley, Charles. A Farewell. Accessed November 25, 2015. https://www.inspirationalstories.com/poems/a-farewell-charles-kingsley-poem/.

Kramer, Kenneth. *Redeeming Time: T.S. Eliot's Four Quartets*. Cambridge MA: Cowley Publications, 2007, p. 174.

Lamott, Anne. *Almost Everything: Notes on hope*. New York: Random House, 2018.

Meredith, Jane. *Journey to the Dark Goddess: How to return to your soul*. Washington DC: Moon Books, 2011.

Merton, Thomas. *Contemplative Prayer*. Toronto: Random House Canada, 1971.

Metzner, Ralph. *Allies for Awakening: Guidelines for productive and safe experiences with entheogens*. Berkeley: Regent Press, 2015.

Miller, Jerome. *In the Throe of Wonder: Intimations of the sacred in a post-modern world*. Albany NY: State University of New York Press, 1992.

Miller, Jerome. *The Way of Suffering: A geography of crisis*. Washington DC: Georgetown University Press, 1988.

Myss, Caroline. *Entering the Castle: Finding the inner path to God and your soul's purpose.* New York: Atria,2007.

Stuhlman, Gunther, Ed. *The Diary of Anaïs Nin.* Volume 3, 1939-1944. New York: Harcourt, 1971.

Pearson, Carol. *Awakening the Heroes Within: Twelve archetypes to help us find ourselves and transform our world.* New York: Harper, 1991.

Pollan, Michael. *How to Change Your Mind: What the new science of psychedelics teaches us about consciousness, dying, addiction, depression and transcendence.* New York:Penguin, 2018.

Ray, Reggie. *Touching Enlightenment.* Accessed August 20, 2017. https://www.beliefnet.com/faiths/buddhism/2006/05/touching-enlightenment.aspx.

Remen, Rachel Naomi. *Kitchen Table Wisdom: Stories that heal.* Tenth Anniversary Edition, New York: Penguin, 2006.

Rilke, Rainer Maria. *Letters to a Young Poet.* New York: Random, 2004.

St. John of the Cross. *Dark Night of the Soul.* Mineola NY: Dover Publications, 2003.

Shabad, Peter. *Despair and the Return of Hope: Echoes of mourning in psychotherapy.* Lanham, MA: Rowan and Littlefield, 2001.

Shaw, Martin. "Small Gods." Accessed November 13, 2017.
https://drmartinshaw.com/essays/.

Silko, Leslie Marmon. *Ceremony*. New York: Penguin, 1997.

Singer, Michael. (2015, June 4). In: Jennifer D'Angelo
Friedman, The Surrender Experiment: How one yogi
found life's perfection. Yoga Journal.

Solnit, Rebecca. *Hope in the Dark: Untold histories, wild
possibilities*. Chicago: Haymarket, 2016.

Smith, Rodney. *Awakening: A paradigm shift of the heart*.
Boulder CO: Shambala, 2014.

Ulanov, Ann Belford. *The Feminine in Jungian Psychology
and in Christian Theology*. Evanston IL: Northwestern
University Press, 1971.

Viorst, Judith. *Necessary Losses: The loves, illusions,
dependencies and impossible expectations that all of
us have to give up in order to grow*. New York:
Simon and Shuster, 2010.

Walker, Alice. *In Search of our Mothers' Gardens*. New
York: Open Road Media, 2011.

Whyte, David. *Consolations: The Solace, Nourishment and
Underlying Meaning of Everyday Words*. Langley
WA: Many Rivers Press, 2015.

Wilber, Ken. *Integral Spirituality: A startling new role for
religion in the modern and postmodern world*.
Boulder CO: Shambala, 2007.

Winnicott, D.W. *Home is Where We Start From: Essays by a Psychoanalyst.* New York: Norton, 1990.

Woodman, Marion. *Conscious Femininity.* Toronto: Inner City Books, 1993.

Wright, Susan and Carol MacKinnon. *Leadership Alchemy: The magic of the leader coach.* Toronto: TCP Publications, 2003.

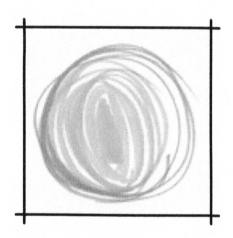

Contributors

I am incredibly grateful to the friends who have so openly and bravely agreed to tell their dark night stories and have them interpreted by me and then witnessed by you, the reader. Through my own writing, I have seen how important it is to tell my story, to see it from the outside in, to be an observer of it rather than a victim. I have become an outspoken advocate for getting our stories out there, whether they are written, sung, drawn, spoken or danced. It is one of the central ways to build our capacity for navigating these life-changing journeys.

With that in mind, I asked the storytellers about their experience of having their stories heard and retold. They kindly agreed to give me some thoughts. I hope these perspectives are an encouragement to give voice to your own encounter with the dark night.

Dirk:

The cathartic effect of writing the story was the strongest reaction I've had to my view of me and my problem since I had the stroke. It has not made living the dark night called life a better experience, but it allows me to take a 'looking in from outside' view of my life, and as such has had a slightly lightening effect. No one here really wants to hear my story any more so having this outlet has made a difference.

Charlotte:

What has given me pause for thought from retelling my story is the deepening of my inner conversation. The process has engendered revelations, especially engaging in defining the difference between loss and depression. Reading my story now, there seems to be nothing but sadness and loss. However, there are some glimmerings of how comedy and tragedy live in me side-by-side as part of the whole, and joy is always present no matter how grave the losses.

Nadine:

When Susan casually made an open invitation in a group about being interviewed, I was immediately interested. I like to contribute and the idea of sharing my story was provocative. The interview was light, playful and meaningful mostly because of Susan's trustworthiness, openness, listening, and the setting on Granville Island. As the words appeared on paper, the reality started to sink in. Although I had journaled about it through the years, it had neither been written as a complete story nor been exposed to other eyes and ears. As much as I appreciated the

238

intimacy and vulnerability of the experience, rare in my solo life, doubt, fear and shame swirled through my mind when I imagined it in a book. Then, a deeper awareness emerged that the story is just a story that I can and have changed each time I tell it, that there is privilege and gratitude from shining a flashlight into the dark night and that there is deep learning, affirmation and meaning from leaning into the mystery of my interior life.

Mary:

Susan's interview gave me the chance to say YES to my dark night experience. I claimed my bravery, confusion, resilience, and openness to both my painful and joyous experience. Through storytelling I gained perspective, discovered new meanings, found bits of gold I hadn't noticed before, and gained deeper satisfaction. I'm honoured to be part of Susan's gift to the world!

Donald:

When I think about telling my story, I am reminded of the value of having difficult conversations and how they can move us forward. I realize I am ultimately responsible to initiate those conversations. It may be painful at the time, but it helps me see myself as others see me and make the appropriate choices. It's really all about open and honest communication in relationships.

Sheila:

There really is something to be said for repetition, articulating that which is vaguely known and understood but strongly operating within us. Retelling my story has been a catalyst to seeing my whole dark night experience in a different way, standing back and seeing a bigger picture, the weft and the weave of what I have been feeling/experiencing and also the huge step to have it witnessed by others. I think it's empowering and freeing. It's like looking at a jigsaw puzzle from five meters away rather than five centimeters where all you can see are the tiny pieces. It makes me think there is something in this work about helping people write these stories, not only to see their own puzzle from a distance but to stand further back and realize there is really one huge jigsaw puzzle that is all our stories, the foundational art of our lived experience.

Made in the USA
Monee, IL
24 October 2020